v021718
pc: 142
ISBN Printed Book: 9781944607258
ISBN eBook: 9781944607265

Adobe Presenter 11:
The Essentials

"Skills and Drills" Learning

Kevin Siegel & Jennie Ruby

"Skills and Drills" Learning

Contents

About This Book
The Authors... vi
Book Conventions.. vi
Confidence Checks vii
System Requirements vii
Data Files (Presenter Project Assets).. viii
 Download the Data Files... viii
How Software Updates Affect This Book.. ix
Acknowledgments ix
Contacting IconLogic.. ix

Preface
Adobe Presenter's Role in eLearning.. 2
Designing Slides Within PowerPoint 3
Fonts and Learning 4
Planning eLearning Projects 7
eLearning Budgeting Considerations.. 8
Scripts for Software Demonstrations 10
Storyboarding for Soft Skills 11
 Storyboard Confidence Check 12
 Suggested Answers 14
The Value of Audio 16

Module 1: Presenter Basics
The Interface.. 20
 Explore an Existing Presentation.. 20
 Publishing Confidence Check.. 27
Characters 30
 Insert and Resize a Character 30
 Characters Confidence Check 32
Scenes.. 34
 Create a Scene 34
 Characters Confidence Check 35

Module 2: Audio
Voiceover Scripts 38
 Add Slides Notes 38
 Voiceover Confidence Check 40
Recording Voiceover Audio.. 41
 Record Voiceover Audio... 41
Importing Audio 44
 Import and Review an Audio File 44
 Importing Audio Confidence Check 46
Editing Audio 47
 Add Silence and Delete Audio 47
 Control Audio Volume 50
 Audio Editing Confidence Check.. 51

Module 3: Video and Pictures
Slide Video 54
 Add a Video to a Slide... 54
 Edit an Imported Video 57
 Videos Confidence Check... 58
Sidebar Video 59
 Import a Sidebar Video 59

Pictures 61
    Import a Picture Onto a Slide 61
    Images Confidence Check 63

Module 4: Interactive eLearning
Interactions 66
    Insert a Word Search Interaction 66
    Interaction Confidence Check 68
    Manage a Slide 71
Scenario Interactions 73
    Create a Scenario Interaction 73
    Scenario Confidence Check 76
    Create a Hyperlink 78

Module 5: Quizzing
Creating Quizzes 82
    Add a Quiz 82
    Insert a Graded Question 86
    Question Slide Confidence Check 88
    Add a Survey Question 89

Module 6: Reporting Data
Preparing a Lesson for an LMS 92
    Set Quiz Reporting Options 93
    Create a Manifest File 96
    Publish a Content Package 98
    LMS Confidence Check 99
Uploading to an LMS 100
    Create an Inquisiq LMS Account 101
    Create an LMS Course 103
    Attach a Lesson to a Course 104
    Create an LMS Catalog 106
    Attach a Course to a Catalog 107
    Test an eLearning Course 108

Module 7: Finishing Touches
Themes 112
    Apply a Theme 112
    Customize a Theme 114
    Themes Confidence Check 115
Settings 116
    Edit the Presentation Settings 116
    Add a Presenter 118
    Modify Sidebar Presenter Info 119
Managing Slides 120
    Assign a Presenter to Slides 120
    Slide Manager Confidence Check 122
Packaging 124
    Create a Package 124
    Your Final Confidence Check 125

Notes

iCONLOGiC
"Skills and Drills" Learning

About This Book

This Section Contains Information About:

- The Authors, page vi
- Book Conventions, page vi
- Confidence Checks, page vii
- System Requirements, page vii
- Data Files (Presenter Project Assets), page viii
- How Software Updates Affect This Book, page ix
- Acknowledgments, page ix
- Contacting IconLogic, page ix

The Authors

Kevin Siegel is the founder and president of IconLogic, Inc. He has written hundreds of step-by-step computer training books on applications such as *Adobe Captivate, Articulate Storyline, Adobe RoboHelp, Adobe Presenter, Adobe Technical Communication Suite, Adobe Dreamweaver, Adobe InDesign, Microsoft Office, Microsoft PowerPoint, QuarkXPress,* and *TechSmith Camtasia.*

Kevin spent five years in the U.S. Coast Guard as an award-winning photojournalist and has three decades' experience as a print publisher, technical writer, instructional designer, and eLearning developer. He is a certified technical trainer, a veteran classroom instructor, and a frequent speaker at trade shows and conventions.

Kevin holds multiple certifications. He is a Certified Technical Trainer (CTT), and a Certified Online Training Professional (COTP). You can reach Kevin at **ksiegel@iconlogic.com**.

Jennie Ruby is a veteran eLearning developer, a Certified Technical Trainer (CTT), a Certified Online Training Professional (COTP), and author of *Effective Writing for Curriculum Development, Microsoft Access, An Introduction, Editing with Microsoft Word, Introduction to Copyediting, Professional Proofreading, Writing for the Web, Advanced Grammar, Substantive Editing, Editing with Acrobat, Mastering Track Changes in Word, Adobe Presenter 9: The Essentials, Adobe Presenter 10: The Essentials,* and *Managing the Review Process with Acrobat.*

Jennie has an M.A. from George Washington University and is a Certified Technical Trainer (CompTIA). She is a training professional with nearly 20 years of experience in classroom and online training as well as eLearning script development. Jennie holds multiple certifications from companies such as CompTIA. You can reach Jennie at **jenruby@aol.com**.

Book Conventions

At IconLogic, we believe that learners learn by doing. With that simple concept in mind, IconLogic books are created by trainers/authors with years of experience training adult learners. Before IconLogic books, our instructors rarely found a book that was perfect for a classroom setting. If the book was beautiful, odds were that the text was too small to read and hard to follow. If the text in a book was the right size, the quality of exercises left something to be desired.

Finally tiring of using inadequate materials, our instructors started teaching without any books at all. Years ago we had classroom students ask if the in-class instruction came from a book. If so, they said they'd buy the book. That sparked an idea. Our authors began writing books that mirrored the way instructors taught live classes. Classroom lessons are always short and to the point... no fluff. That methodology is used in this book and every IconLogic training guide.

This book has been divided into several modules. Since each module builds on lessons learned in a previous module, it is recommend that you complete each module in succession. During every module, you will be guided through lessons step by step. Instructions for you to follow will look like this:

❐ instructions for you to follow will look like this

If you are expected to type anything or if something is important, it will be set in bold type like this:

❐ type **9** into the text field

When you are asked to press a key on your keyboard, the instruction will look like this:

❐ press [**shift**]

We hope you enjoy this book. If you have any comments or questions, feel free to email IconLogic directly at **info@iconlogic.com**. There is additional contact information for IconLogic on page ix of this section.

Confidence Checks

As you move through the lessons in this book, you will come across the little guy at the right. He indicates a Confidence Check. Throughout each module you will be guided through hands-on, step-by-step exercises. But at some point you'll have to fend for yourself. That is where Confidence Checks come in. Please be sure to complete each of the challenges because some exercises build on completed Confidence Checks.

System Requirements

This book teaches you how to use many, but not all, of the features of Adobe Presenter. The Adobe Presenter software does not come with this book. The software can be downloaded directly from Adobe (**http://www.adobe.com/products/presenter.html**).

While you need to have both **Microsoft PowerPoint** and **Adobe Presenter** installed on your computer prior to starting the hands-on activities presented in this book, you **do not** need to purchase Presenter to learn Presenter; the free 30-day trial version of the software can be downloaded via the link above. There are few limitations to the Presenter trial and it will continue to work for 30 days from the day you first start the program. However, eLearning lessons that you create using the trial version of Presenter will no longer open once the trial period expires. (Any projects you create with the trial will be available to edit and publish once you license the software.)

Here are Adobe's system requirements for installing and using Adobe Presenter 11.

System requirements for Working with Presenter: Windows 7, Windows 8.1, or Windows 10; Intel Core 2 Duo or AMD Phenom II processor (Intel Core i3 or faster recommended); 2GB of RAM (4GB or more recommended); 6GB of available hard-disk space for installation; 5GB space required during usage; 1024x768 display (1280x720 display with OpenGL 2.1-compatible dedicated graphics card highly recommended); Recent versions of Internet Explorer, Firefox, or Safari; Adobe Reader 9 software and above for viewing PDF files created with Adobe Presenter; Windows Media Player; Adobe Flash Player 9 or later for viewing multimedia content; Microsoft PowerPoint 2010, 2013, or 2016.

System requirement for viewing Presenter content: Internet Explorer 10 or Edge on Windows 10; Firefox 4.x or later; Chrome 37 or later, Safari 6 or later; Adobe Reader 9 or later for viewing the PDF created using Adobe Presenter 11. HTML5 content on the iPad; Safari 6 or newer. HTML5 content on the Android; Chrome 37 or newer.

Languages: While Presenter is available in multiple languages, the English version is shown in this book.

Data Files (Presenter Project Assets)

You're probably chomping at the bit, ready to dive into Presenter and begin creating eLearning lessons. Not so fast. Do you have sample projects to work with? What about graphics? Do you have some audio files to use as voiceovers? No? No worries. We've got everything you need—we call them data files—and they can be downloaded from the IconLogic website for free.

Student Activity: Download the Data Files

1. Download the student data files necessary to use this book.

   ❐ start a web browser and go to the following web address:
   http://www.iconlogic.com/pc
   ❐ under the **Adobe Presenter Data Files** section, click the
   Presenter 11: The Essentials link

   On most web browsers, a dialog box appears asking if you want to Save, Run or Open the file. The goal is to save the file to your computer. It doesn't matter where you save the file, provided you can find it in a moment to execute it.

2. Save the Presenter11Data.exe file to your computer. (After the file downloads, you can close the web browser.)

3. Unzip the **Presenter11Data** files to your computer.

   ❐ find the **Presenter11Data.exe** file you just downloaded to your computer
   ❐ double-click the file to open the **WinZip Self-Extractor**
   ❐ confirm **C:** appears in the **Unzip to folder** area

   Note: You can **Browse** and change the **Unzip to folder** location if you are not permitted to install files on your C drive.

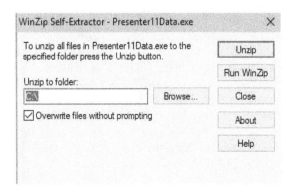

❑ click the **Unzip** button

You are notified that several files are unzipped.

❑ click the **OK** button and then click the **Close** button to close Self-Extractor

Before starting the lessons in this book, it's a good idea to review "How Software Updates Affect This Book" on page ix.

How Software Updates Affect This Book

This book was written specifically to teach you how to use Adobe Presenter version 11. At the time that this book was written, Presenter **11.1** was the latest and greatest version of the Presenter software available from Adobe.

With each major release of Presenter, our intention is to write a new book to support that version and to make it available within 30-60 days of the software being released by Adobe. From time to time, Adobe makes service releases/patches of Presenter available for customers that fix bugs or add functionality. The patched versions might be called Presenter **11.11** or **11.2**. Usually these updates are minor (bug fixes) and have little or no impact on the lessons presented in this book. However, Adobe could make significant changes to the way Presenter looks or behaves, even with minor patches. (Such was the case when Adobe updated its Adobe Captivate from version 5 to 5.5—about a dozen features were added, and a few panels/pods were renamed, throwing readers of those books into a tizzy.)

Since it is not possible for us to recall and update printed books, instructions you are asked to follow in this book may not exactly match the patched/updated version of Presenter that you are using. If something on your screen does not match what is in the book, please visit the book errata page on my website (http://www.iconlogic.com/skills-drills-workbooks/errata-pages.html). If an Adobe software update has altered something that impacts the lessons in this book, we will address the issues on that page as they are brought to our attention.

Acknowledgments

AJ Walther contributed heavily to the Preface of this book (beginning on page 1). Specifically, she wrote the sections on "Designing Slides Within PowerPoint" on page 3, and "Fonts and Learning" on page 4.

We would also like to thank **Margie Maulone** for her good humor and consulting on the content of the medical scenario (page 73).

Contacting IconLogic

Phone: 410.956.4949
Web: www.iconlogic.com
Email: info@iconlogic.com
Facebook: https://www.facebook.com/IconLogicInc/

Notes

iCONLOGiC

"Skills and Drills" Learning

Rank Your Skills

Before starting this book, complete the skills assessment on the next page.

Skills Assessment

How This Assessment Works

Ten course objectives for *Adobe Presenter 11: The Essentials* are listed below. **Before starting the book**, review each objective and rank your skills using the scale next to each objective. A rank of ① means **No Confidence** in the skill. A rank of ⑤ means **Total Confidence**. After you've completed this assessment, work through the entire book. **After finishing the book**, review each objective and rank your skills now that you've completed the book. Most people see dramatic improvements in the second assessment after completing the lessons in this book.

Before-Class Skills Assessment

1. I can Preview a Presentation. ① ② ③ ④ ⑤
2. I can add video to a Presentation. ① ② ③ ④ ⑤
3. I can add a Scenario to a Presentation. ① ② ③ ④ ⑤
4. I can add Characters to a Presentation. ① ② ③ ④ ⑤
5. I can Publish a Presentation as a PDF. ① ② ③ ④ ⑤
6. I can add a Quiz to a Presentation. ① ② ③ ④ ⑤
7. I know how to upload a Presentation to an LMS. ① ② ③ ④ ⑤
8. I know what SCORM stands for. ① ② ③ ④ ⑤
9. I can add an Interaction to a slide. ① ② ③ ④ ⑤
10. I can edit a Presenter Theme. ① ② ③ ④ ⑤

After-Class Skills Assessment

1. I can Preview a Presentation. ① ② ③ ④ ⑤
2. I can add video to a Presentation. ① ② ③ ④ ⑤
3. I can add a Scenario to a Presentation. ① ② ③ ④ ⑤
4. I can add Characters to a Presentation. ① ② ③ ④ ⑤
5. I can Publish a Presentation as a PDF. ① ② ③ ④ ⑤
6. I can add a Quiz to a Presentation. ① ② ③ ④ ⑤
7. I know how to upload a Presentation to an LMS. ① ② ③ ④ ⑤
8. I know what SCORM stands for. ① ② ③ ④ ⑤
9. I can add an Interaction to a slide. ① ② ③ ④ ⑤
10. I can edit a Presenter Theme. ① ② ③ ④ ⑤

iCONLOGiC
"Skills and Drills" Learning

Preface

This Section Covers:

- Adobe Presenter's Role in eLearning, page 2
- Designing Slides Within PowerPoint, page 3
- Fonts and Learning, page 4
- Planning eLearning Projects, page 7
- eLearning Budgeting Considerations, page 8
- Scripts for Software Demonstrations, page 10
- Storyboarding for Soft Skills, page 11
- The Value of Audio, page 16

Adobe Presenter's Role in eLearning

According to Adobe, the Presenter software "makes it easy to turn passive PowerPoint content into video presentations, product demonstrations, and training videos." Nice, but what does passive PowerPoint content mean?

It's likely that you've used Microsoft PowerPoint to create at least a few presentations. PowerPoint is a great program and you can create some compelling presentations with the tool. Unfortunately, the vast majority of presentations created with PowerPoint are terrible. You've likely seen your share of these terrible presentations: slides with a main headline, perhaps a subhead and a bunch of bullets. Worse: slides with a headline, a bunch of bullets, a bunch of images (lots of images) and slide elements that fly all over the place. We have a name for those kinds of presentations: *Death by PowerPoint*.

When learners are presented with a series of PowerPoint slides that are nothing more than slides with a headline, a bunch of bullets and a button to click through, learners will simply click from one slide to the next. There's typically little or no interaction on the slides beyond clicking forward and back buttons. And there's definitely no way to measure learner comprehension of the content because PowerPoint does not have the ability to include a quiz.

When the time comes to deliver content created in PowerPoint to learners across the globe, learners either need to have PowerPoint installed on their computers or download the PowerPoint player from Microsoft. While you can upload a PowerPoint presentation into a Learning Management System (LMS) as a course asset, there is no way to make the presentation SCORM or AICC compliant from within PowerPoint so that learner progress can be tracked by the LMS.

The bottom line is that while PowerPoint is great at creating presentations, it's not a very good eLearning development tool.

Along comes Adobe Presenter which, at its core, is simply a PowerPoint add-in. Once you've installed Presenter, you might not find it via the Start button on the Taskbar. Instead, after installing Presenter on your computer and then starting PowerPoint, you'll find that there's a new ribbon to be found: Adobe Presenter.

The first image below shows the entire Microsoft PowerPoint 2016 Ribbon (the Adobe Presenter tab is located at the right of the Ribbon). The second image shows Adobe Presenter and its tools.

In the image of the Presenter ribbon above, you can see that there aren't that many tools. While the lack of tools may lead you to believe that Presenter doesn't perform many tricks, you'll soon learn how deceptive the streamlined Presenter interface truly is. At the far left of the Presenter ribbon, you'll find recording tools for both audio and video. As you move right, you'll see tools for adding interactions, characters, and more. You'll be using many of the tools (along with the standard PowerPoint tools) you see on the ribbon as you move through the lessons in this book.

Designing Slides Within PowerPoint

As mentioned earlier, working with Presenter means you also need to work within PowerPoint. It stands to reason that the better your PowerPoint presentation looks, the more likely it is that your learners will want to consume the content you publish.

We saw a guy the other day wearing a t-shirt that read, "Guns don't kill people, people kill people." Often the same holds true for PowerPoint presentations. "PowerPoint doesn't kill presentations, people kill presentations."

It's easy to point the finger at PowerPoint for making office meetings unsuccessful and presentations a snore, but the truth is that poor design is really to blame.

The good news is that you don't have to be a seasoned designer to produce beautiful and effective PowerPoint presentations. Here are a few tips to get you started:

- ❏ There are certainly occasions when a bullet really is the most successful way to convey an idea. However, just because PowerPoint defaults to using a bulleted format doesn't mean that you should go with the flow and present all your information with a bullet in front of it.

- ❏ Try splitting the bullets up into separate slides with a single image to illustrate each point, or forgo the text altogether and replace it with a chart, diagram, or other informative image.

- ❏ It is not necessary to have every bit of information you cover up on the slide. Encourage your audience to listen and, if necessary, take notes based on what you say, not what is on the slide.

- ❏ Nothing says "High School Presentation Circa 1997" quite like a dancing animated image clumsily plopped on a rainbow gradient background with a big, garish WordArt title (complete with myriad animation effects).

- ❏ Keep in mind that PowerPoint presentations are plentiful—particularly bad ones. Trust us, your learner will not be impressed with how many moving, colorful parts each slide contains.

- ❏ Consider taking more of a photographic approach to the images you use. PowerPoint comes preloaded with photograph clip art images you can use. If you find the selection isn't enough to suit your needs, try looking online for stock photos. There are many free sites, but keep in mind that to save time and frustration (and improve on the selection and quality) you might want to set aside a budget to pay for images.

Fonts and Learning

There is no denying that the most important thing about eLearning is solid content. But could you be inadvertently making your content harder to read and understand by using the wrong fonts? Is good font selection really important? Read on to discover the many surprising ways fonts can affect your content.

Some Fonts Read Better On-Screen

eCommerce Consultant Dr. Ralph F. Wilson did a study back in 2001 to determine if serif fonts (fonts with little lines on the tops and bottoms of characters such as Times New Roman) or sans serif fonts (those without lines, such as Arial) were more suited to being read on computer monitors. His study concluded that although Times New Roman is easily read in printed materials, the lower resolution of monitors (72 dpi vs 180 dpi or higher) makes it much more difficult to read in digital format. Arial 12 pt was pitted against Times New Roman 12pt with respondents finding the sans serif Arial font more readable at a rate of 2-to-1.

Lorem ipsum frangali puttuto rigali fortuitous confulence magficati alorem. Lorem ipsum frangali puttuto rigali fortuitous confulence magficati alorem.	Lorem ipsum frangali puttuto rigali fortuitous confulence magficati alorem. Lorem ipsum frangali puttuto rigali fortuitous confulence magficati alorem.
Times New Roman 12 pt	Arial 12 pt
520	1123
32%	68%

Wilson also tested the readability of Arial vs. Verdana on computer screens and found that in font sizes greater than 10 pt, Arial was more readable, whereas Verdana was more readable in font sizes 10 pt and smaller.

So should you stop using Times New Roman in your eLearning lessons? Not completely. For instance, you can still use Times New Roman for text content that is not expected to be skimmed over quickly or read in a hurry.

Some Fonts Increase Trust

A 2008 study by Sharath Sasidharan and Ganga Dhanesh for the Association of Information Systems found that typography can affect trust in eCommerce. The study found that to instill trust in online consumers, you should keep it simple: "To the extent possible, particularly for websites that need to engage in financial transactions or collect personal information from their users, the dominant typeface used to present text material should be a serif or sans serif font such as Times New Roman or Arial."

If you feel your eLearning content will be presented to a skeptical audience (or one you've never worked with before), dazzling them with fancy fonts may not be the way to go. We're not saying that you shouldn't use fancy fonts from time to time to break up the monotony of a dry lesson, but consider using such non-standard fonts sparingly. Use the fancy fonts for headings or as accents but not for the bulk of your text.

The Readability of Fonts Affects Participation

A study done at the University of Michigan in 2008 on typecase in instructions found that the ease with which a font in instructional material is read can have an impact on the perceived skill level needed to complete a task.

The study found that if directions are presented in a font that is deemed more difficult to read, "the task will be viewed as being difficult, taking a long time to complete and perhaps, not even worth trying."

Based upon the aforementioned study by Wilson, it is probably not a good idea to present eLearning material, especially to beginners, in a Times New Roman font, as it may make the information seem too difficult to process or overwhelming.

Most Popular Fonts

We polled our "Skills & Drills" newsletter readers and asked which fonts they tended to use in eLearning. Here is a list of the most popular fonts:

- ❑ Verdana
- ❑ Helvetica
- ❑ Arial
- ❑ Calibri
- ❑ Times
- ❑ Palatino
- ❑ Times New Roman
- ❑ Century Schoolbook (for print)

Fonts and Personas

If you are creating eLearning for business professionals, you might want to use a different font in your design than you would if you were creating eLearning for high school students. But what font would you use if you wanted to convey a feeling of happiness? Formality? Cuddliness?

In a study (funded by Microsoft) by A. Dawn Shaikh, Barbara S. Chaparro and Doug Fox, the perceived personality traits of fonts were categorized. The table below shows the top three fonts for each personality objective.

	Top Three		
Stable	TNR	Arial	Cambria
Flexible	Kristen	Gigi	Rage Italic
Conformist	Courier New	TNR	Arial
Polite	Monotype Corsiva	TNR	Cambria
Mature	TNR	Courier New	Cambria
Formal	TNR	Monotype Corsiva	Georgia
Assertive	Impact	Rockwell Xbold	Georgia
Practical	Georgia	TNR	Cambria
Creative	Gigi	Kristen	Rage Italic
Happy	Kristen	Gigi	Comic Sans
Exciting	Gigi	Kristen	Rage Italic
Attractive	Monotype Corsiva	Rage Italic	Gigi
Elegant	Monotype Corsiva	Rage Italic	Gigi
Cuddly	Kristen	Gigi	Comic Sans
Feminine	Gigi	Monotype Corsiva	Kristen
Unstable	Gigi	Kristen	Rage Italic
Rigid	Impact	Courier New	Agency FB
Rebel	Gigi	Kristen	Rage Italic
Rude	Impact	Rockwell Xbold	Agency FB
Youthful	Kristen	Gigi	Comic Sans
Casual	Kristen	Comic Sans	Gigi
Passive	Kristen	Gigi	Comic Sans
Impractical	Gigi	Rage Italic	Kristen
Unimaginative	Courier New	Arial	Consolas
Sad	Impact	Courier New	Agency FB
Dull	Courier New	Consolas	Verdana
Unattractive	Impact	Courier New	Rockwell Xbold
Plain	Courier New	Impact	Rockwell Xbold
Coarse	Impact	Rockwell Xbold	Courier New
Masculine	Impact	Rockwell Xbold	Courier New

Source: http://usabilitynews.org/perception-of-fonts-perceived-personality-traits-and-uses/

Planning eLearning Projects

By the time you finish the last lesson in this book, you should be able to use Presenter to create some compelling, technically sound eLearning lessons. However, just because you will soon be able to publish technically sound content does not necessarily mean you will go out and create *good* eLearning lessons. If you want to create good, useful lessons, you have to plan ahead. Before creating an eLearning lesson using Presenter, you should ask yourself the following questions:

❑ Who is my audience? Are you training children or business professionals? The images you use and the interactions you include will need to take your audience into consideration.

❑ Is my audience hearing challenged? If so, you'll need to include closed captions.

❑ Do I want my lessons to contain images and background music? If so, where will I get them? While Presenter comes with a ton of free assets, those assets may not be enough. In that case, you'll need a reliable source for gathering additional assets. For instance, we use www.BigStock.com for many of the images we use in our eLearning lessons. We also rely heavily on eLearning resources such as www.eLearningBrothers.com for assets appropriate for eLearning.

❑ Do you need to capture learner data? If so, you'll likely need a Learning Management System (LMS). You'll learn more about LMSs beginning on page 92.

When planning projects, keep in mind that the most useful lessons contain the following basic elements:

❑ Title slide (telling the learner what they are going to learn)

❑ Lesson slides containing narration, music and other sound effects

❑ Images and animations

❑ As much interactivity as possible (via interactions and buttons)

❑ A quiz (to gauge the effectiveness of the lesson)

❑ An ending slide (reviewing what the learner learned)

Above all, remember the mantra used in the best training courses world-wide: *tell them what you're going to teach them, teach them, and then tell them what you taught them*. If your eLearning content created with Presenter takes this mantra into account, there's a very good chance you'll not just create eLearning content, you'll create successful eLearning content.

eLearning Budgeting Considerations

Many new eLearning developers underestimate the time needed to produce eLearning content with PowerPoint and Presenter. The following table should help.

Project Size	Number of Production Hours
Small Projects (1-25 slides)	1-4 hours
Medium Projects (26-79 slides)	5-7 hours
Large Projects (80-150 slides)	8-10 hours
Bloated Projects (more than 150 slides)	Consider splitting lessons this large into smaller presentations.

We bet you're wondering what "production" means, especially considering the fact that most of the projects you create will likely be in the large category (80-150 slides) and take you, on average, 10 hours to produce.

What Production Does Not Include

To begin, let's consider what "production" does **not** include. An effective one-hour eLearning course will not play for 60 consecutive minutes. Given today's distractions, the perfect playtime for any one eLearning lesson is between 3-7 minutes (a 5-minute playtime is ideal). Given a 5-minute playtime, that means that a 60-minute eLearning course would consist of 12, 5-minute lessons.

Before you can even think about creating an eLearning course, you'll need a script and/or storyboard (see page 10). A general rule of thumb is that it takes up to 40 hours to write every one hour of eLearning. Depending on how fast you write, you could easily save some time here (if you're a fast writer). However, you could also double those hours if you're new to creating eLearning content (or perhaps you simply write slowly).

If you're going to include voiceover audio (see page 38), you'll first need to write a voiceover script. Many writers budget at least 50% of the time it takes to write a standard script to write a voiceover script. And some writers say that writing a voiceover script is just as difficult, if not more difficult, than writing a step-by-step eLearning script. To be safe, you should budget the same number of hours to write a voiceover script as you budgeted for the eLearning script.

Production won't include creating a PowerPoint template, a completed shell project that you will use as the basis of all of your projects. It's not difficult to create a template, but it will take time. An ideal template contains placeholders, an introduction slide, transitional slides, a conclusion slide, and a quiz placeholder. We typically budget up to 10 hours to create a project template.

What Production Does Include

A single interactive PowerPoint/Presenter eLearning lesson could take you up to 10 hours to produce. What's part of the production process?

You'll spend a lot of time working with each and every PowerPoint slide. Adding the content and the images will take time. Beyond the slide content and images, you'll be adding interactive objects (such as buttons and interactions). You'll also likely be adding audio to the presentation (if you're lucky, the audio won't need any editing... but it's more likely you'll need to spend time editing the audio's waveform).

To measure the success of your eLearning lesson, you'll need a quiz. It's going to take time to write the questions, the answers, and the distractors. If you've never written questions and answers for a quiz, it's not as easy as you think. And it's going to take time. You should budget 15-20 minutes per question (the average eLearning lesson should contain no more than 10 questions).

During the production process, you'll be publishing the project into any one of several output formats and possibly uploading those files to a web server or LMS. You will be testing the lessons for scoring or interactivity errors. After that, you'll need to fix problems you run across (and there will likely be plenty of problems that need to be fixed). After fixing those problems, you'll need to republish, repost and then retest.

Add it all up, and your budget looks something like this (keep in mind that the timing below does not include the time it will take to record and edit your own voiceover audio):

- ❐ 40-80 hours to write an eLearning script or create the storyboard to support 12, five-minute lessons for a one-hour course.

- ❐ 120 hours to edit, produce and test 12, five-minute lessons for a one-hour eLearning course.

- ❐ 40-80 hours to write a narration script to be used by your narrator.

Scripts for Software Demonstrations

When developing eLearning for software demonstrations or simulations (using eLearning tools like Adobe Captivate), it's a great idea to begin with a script... a detailed list of step-by-step instructions. When we have created text-based eLearning scripts, or received them from clients, we've generally seen them in two flavors: paragraphs and tables.

Scripts in Paragraph Format: If you are creating a script for eLearning, your text should be formatted in a way that is easy to follow. You can format the script in paragraphs, but you will need to clearly label the parts. You may find that formatted paragraphs are all you need. However, we recommend a table or grid format for a script that will be developed into eLearning.

- ☐ **Step Number**

- ☐ **Screen:** Display the document

- ☐ **Action:** Move the cursor to the Format menu and click Format

- ☐ **Caption:** Click Format

- ☐ **Voiceover:** Now let's open the Format menu to get started with formatting the document.

Scripts in Table Format: Below is a picture of a sample script used to create an Adobe Captivate eLearning lesson. The script was created in Microsoft Word. You'll find the script among the assets within the Presenter11Data folder (the file is called **SampleScript**).

Sample Script for Recording Captivate eLearning

Movie Name: Print a NotePad File with Landscape Orientation

Step	Screen	Action to be Taken by Captivate Developer	Caption Text	Narrator Says
1)	A NotePad file should be open prior to recording. You can start NotePad by choose Start > Run and typing notepad. Any open NotePad document can be used for this simulation.	Pull a screen shot of the NotePad file do not click anything. This slide will contain some introductory narrative.	During this lesson you will learn how to print a NotePad document	During this lesson you will learn how to print a NotePad document in Landscape Orientation.
2)	A NotePad file is open. Nothing should be <u>selected</u> and no menus should be open.	Click the **File** menu	First, let's display the Print dialog box. Choose **File > Print**.	To begin, let's display the Print dialog box by choosing the Print command from the File menu.
3)	The File menu is open.	Click the **Print** command	Select the Print command	
4)	Print Dialog Box with NotePad in the background	Select the HP4000 printer icon	The Print Dialog Box appears. Before you can print, you will need to select the correct printer. Select the **HP4000** printer icon.	The Print Dialog Box appears. Before you can print, you will need to select the correct printer. Select the HP4000 printer.

IconLogic Sample eLearning Script

Storyboarding for Soft Skills

When the training objective is a soft skill, such as how to interact with others in the workplace or how to comply with legally required behavior, there may be no step-by-step process to spell out. Instead, you have to describe and demonstrate the behavior in a way that engages the learner. This is where the screen writing part of writing training materials comes into play.

You can present soft skills, which is typically what Adobe Presenter is used to create, through slides or videos. Either way, the material must be both clear and engaging.

Here is a typical plot-line for soft skills training.

- ❏ Statement of a real-world problem, challenge, or requirement

- ❏ Illustration of what happens on failure

- ❏ Demonstration and description of how to succeed

- ❏ Confidence check or evaluation

A visual storyboard allows you to plan what is pictured or acted out as well as what is said for each slide or scene. Even if you are not an artist, you can sketch the basics of the characters, setting, and behavior for each scene. In fact, take a look at the image below. We think that you will agree that the image is not a work of art. Nevertheless, you can tell that it depicts two people meeting in the reception area of an office. Even if the images mean something entirely different to you, you will be writing the script for these images in the Confidence Check that follows.

Slide/ Scene No.	Picture	Voiceover	Action	Dialogue
1				
2				
3				

Storyboard Confidence Check

Here are the visual storyboards for a training unit on how to greet a visitor to your office. Write the script for these scenes. Include a voiceover for each scene, briefly describe the action, and create dialog for the two actors in each scene as well. Some screens will have voiceover only.

Objective:

At the end of this lesson, you will be able to list at least four key behaviors in welcoming a guest to your office. In addition, you will have developed a specific plan for how to do this in your own office setting.

Slide/ Scene No.	Picture	Voiceover	Action	Dialogue
1				
2				
3				
4				
5				
6				

7				
8	**Test Yourself** List at least four things to do when welcoming a guest to your office. 1. _____ 2. _____ 3. _____ 4. _____			
9	**Plan Ahead** 1. Where is your coat closet or rack? _____ 2. Where in your office can you take a visitor to get coffee, soda, or water? _____			

10	Conclusion			

Suggested Answers

1		Don't let social awkwardness keep you from making a good first impression on your client. When a client comes to your office, you'll want to make sure to put them at their ease. Knowing the social niceties and having a plan will help you welcome a guest to your office with confidence. That will put your mind at ease, too!	Ellen and Jeff look uncomfortable and unhappy.	None
2		When you enter the reception area to welcome your guest, make sure to smile.	Ellen enters the reception area and smiles Seeing her smile, Jeff also smiles.	Ellen: Hi! You must be Jeff.
3		Make sure to introduce yourself.	Ellen shakes hands with Jeff	Ellen: I'm Ellen Jones. Its nice to meet you. Jeff: Jeff Barnes. It's nice to meet you too.
4		A proper business handshake is firm and brief. The handshake is a very important part of a proper business greeting.	Focus on handshake	
5		If your guest has an overcoat, offer to take his coat or allow him to hang it on a rack or in a closet.	Ellen takes Jeff's coat and hangs it up in the coat closet.	Ellen: Here's our coat closet. May I take your overcoat? You can retrieve it here after our meeting. Jeff: Yes, thanks!
6		It is also customary to offer your guest coffee, water, or another beverage.	Ellen and Jeff enter the employee lounge, where Ellen points to the coffee and soda machines.	Ellen: Would you care for some coffee or a soda? Jeff: Oh, no thanks. I'm good.

7		Once you arrive at your office, make sure to offer your guest a chair.	Ellen and Jeff arrive in Ellen's office. Ellen gestures toward the guest chair.	Ellen: Please have a seat right over here.
8	**Test Yourself** List at least four things to do when welcoming a guest to your office. 1. _____ 2. _____ 3. _____ 4. _____	Now that you have seen Ellen welcome Jeff to the office, what did you observe? List here four things you can do to welcome a guest or client into your office.		
9	**Plan Ahead** 1. Where is your coat closet or rack? _____ 2. Where in your office can you take a visitor to get coffee, soda, or water? _____	Use this opportunity to plan how you will welcome clients into your office. Do you have a coat rack or closet? Where can you take your visitor to get coffee, soda, tea, or water?		
10	**Conclusion**	By having a plan for welcoming clients to your office, you will be all set to start each new business relationship on a comfortable basis and create a positive experience for each new client.		

The Value of Audio

You'll learn how to record, import, and edit audio files beginning on page 41. Research has shown that voiceover audio, even if it isn't highly produced, enhances the learning experience when compared to eLearning lessons with no audio. If your budget allows, the ideal way to approach audio is to write a voiceover script and then send the script to a voiceover professional. The cost to work with a professional can vary from state to state and region to region. We've seen audio cost as little as a few pennies per word, to several dollars per word. Still other voiceover professionals don't charge by the word at all, they charge by the page.

If you prefer to record the audio yourself, you do not need to have any prior experience recording audio. Nor do you need to have a deep, radio-personality voice. In fact, regular everyday people record perfectly wonderful audio every day. And you'll soon discover that recording audio (or importing audio files) from within Adobe Presenter is very easy. All you really need to record audio is a microphone either hooked up to your computer or built-in. (While some built-in microphones record audio very well, you'll almost always get better results if you use an external microphone or headset.)

Should Voiceover Audio Match the Screen Text?

We spoke to an eLearning student who relayed a frustrating experience she had with an eLearning lesson. The learner needed information about Cascading Style Sheets. She accessed a training site and played an eLearning demo that explained how to redefine an HTML tag. During the video, the learner found herself both listening to the voiceover audio and reading the text on the screen. She quickly realized that the slide text was identical to the voiceover audio. At about the same time, because she had been trying to figure out whether the voiceover really was the same as the slide text, the learner realized that she had not absorbed some of the content. She also noticed that she could read the text on the screen faster than the narrator, so she turned off the audio and just read the rest of the slide text.

The learner had just experienced first-hand what we have heard from fellow eLearning developers over the years: screen text that is identical to the voiceover narration can be a distraction rather than an added value to the learning process. In fact, the best scenario is to have graphics, animation, or video accompanied by voiceover only—with little or no text on the screen at all. Because learners are trying to pay attention to the visuals, the need to move their eyes to focus on the accompanying screen text is a distraction. Having a voiceover explain the visual enables the learner to absorb the audio and visual information at the same time.

In the end, the learner told us that the decision to turn off the audio was a mistake. She felt that she would have had a better learning experience if she had listened to the audio while focusing on the videos and ignoring the printed captions at the bottom of the screen.

Does that mean your PowerPoint slides should never include text? Of course not. Sometimes screen text is required simply because there is no voiceover or the learner may not have access to the voiceover.

Other times when text should appear on screen are:

❑ When there is no visual graphic and the caption text is the only information being presented

❑ When the text is closely integrated with the graphics—as labels rather than separate descriptions

---

❐ When the information being covered is complex and benefits from both audio and visual presentation, as with math equations or chemical formulas

❐ When the information may be needed over time, as in instructions for a learning exercise where the learner may need to repeatedly refer back to the instructions

Ultimately, the use of slide text and voiceovers must be coordinated to enhance, not distract from, the learning experience.

iCONLOGiC

"Skills and Drills" Learning

Module 1: Presenter Basics

In This Module You Will Learn About:

- The Interface, page 20
- Characters, page 30
- Scenes, page 34

And You Will Learn To:

- Explore an Existing Presentation, page 20
- Insert and Resize a Character, page 30
- Create a Scene, page 34

The Interface

As mentioned in the Preface (beginning on page 2), Adobe Presenter is a powerful add-in (or plug-in) to Microsoft PowerPoint. To begin creating a Presenter eLearning lesson, you create a Microsoft PowerPoint presentation as you normally would. When it comes time to add the eLearning component to the PowerPoint presentation, you access the Adobe Presenter tab on the Ribbon.

During the first few activities in this book, you'll have an opportunity to get comfortable within the Presenter tab. To do so, you'll start PowerPoint, open an existing presentation, and explore the Presenter features that have been added to the presentation.

> **Note:** Before moving forward, ensure that you have downloaded and installed the **Presenter11Data** assets as directed in the **About This Book** section of this book (page viii). You'll also need to ensure that you have Microsoft PowerPoint 2010 or newer on your computer (PowerPoint 2016 is shown in the images throughout this book), and that you have installed Adobe Presenter 11. (Review the "System Requirements" section that begins on page vii.)

Student Activity: Explore an Existing Presentation

1. Using Microsoft PowerPoint, open the **AquoSafetyDemo.pptx** file from the **Presenter11Data** folder (not the **AquoSafetyDemo_pptx** folder).

   The **AquoSafetyDemo** presentation was created using standard features found in PowerPoint combined with features found in Adobe Presenter. At first glance, the presentation looks like any other PowerPoint presentation. As mentioned in the Preface of this book, Presenter's relationship within PowerPoint seems subtle, as the only apparent change is the addition of the Adobe Presenter tab on the Ribbon (shown in the red box below).

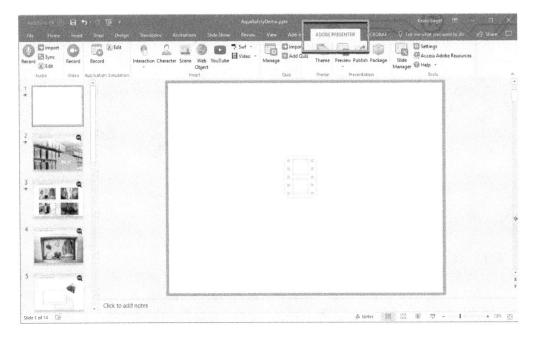

2. Use the Presenter tab on the Ribbon to Preview the eLearning lesson.

☐ on the **PowerPoint Ribbon**, select the **Adobe Presenter** tab

☐ on the **Adobe Presenter** tab, click the **Preview** drop-down menu and choose **Preview Presentation**

Generally speaking, when you click the bottom half of a tool within Microsoft PowerPoint, you'll see a menu of options. If you click the top part of the tool, you'll select the most common command within the menu.

A preview of the presentation appears that will look and behave much as it would if you published the lesson.

☐ spend a few moments going through the presentation

The presentation contains images, videos, audio, and a quiz. You will learn how to work with these kinds of features as you work through the lessons contained within this book.

3. Close the preview.

☐ when finished exploring the preview, click the **OK** button (in the lower right of the preview window)

4. Explore the Audio, Video, and Recording tools.

☐ at the far left of the Adobe Presenter tab, observe the **Audio** group of tools

You'll use the tools found within the Audio group to record, import, and edit audio. You'll work with audio beginning on page 37.

☐ just to the right of the Audio group, observe the **Record Video** tool

The Record Video tool is used to record videos of yourself as the presenter. (Note: You'll need a video camera hooked up to your computer to record a video.)

☐ to the right of Record Video, observe the **Application Simulation** group

The Application Simulation group is only available if you also have the Adobe Captivate software installed on your computer. Captivate is a standalone eLearning development tool that does not rely on Microsoft PowerPoint to create eLearning content. While Presenter and Captivate have some similar features, they are two completely different authoring tools. Since most Adobe Presenter users do not use Adobe Captivate, the Application Simulation group is not covered in this book. If you would like to learn more about the Adobe Captivate software, visit the IconLogic website (www.iconlogic.com) for more information.

5. Observe the Insert group.

   ❑ still working on the Adobe Presenter tab, notice the **Insert** group

   The Insert group has seven tools: Interaction, Character, Scene, Web Object, YouTube, SWF, and Video.

6. Observe the Quiz group.

   ❑ on the Adobe Presenter tab, notice the **Quiz** group

   The Quiz group contains the tools you need to add, import, and manage a quiz. You will learn how to create a Quiz beginning on page 81.

7. Observe the current Theme.

   ❑ from the Adobe Presenter tab, click the **Theme** tool

   The Adobe Presenter Theme Editor opens. You will use the features found within the Editor to control, among other things, the playback controls seen by your learners as they work through each eLearning lesson.

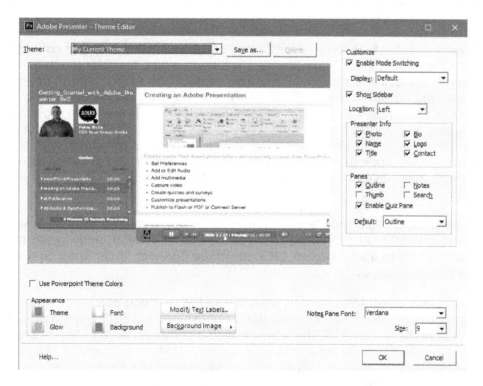

   ❑ click the **Cancel** button

8. Open the Publish Presentation dialog box.

❑ locate the **Presentation** group on the Presenter tab

There are three tools: Preview, Publish, and Package. You have already used one of the Preview options. As you move forward with the lessons presented in this book, you'll learn to both Publish and Package your eLearning lessons so they can be consumed by learners using various devices (PCs running Windows, Macs running the Macintosh operating system, and mobile devices running iOS, such as the iPad).

❑ click the **Publish** tool

The **Publish Presentation** dialog box opens. This is the dialog box you will use once you have finished creating your eLearning lesson using Presenter. To create eLearning content, you need both Microsoft PowerPoint and Adobe Presenter. Before learners can consume your content, you need to publish the content and then upload it to a web server, to Adobe Connect, or to a Learning Management System (LMS).

You can publish your content in SWF or HTML5 format, or in both at once. With either of these formats, Adobe presenter creates multiple, interdependent, output files. All of the published files need to be uploaded to the same location on your web server.

When you publish as SWF, your PowerPoint/Presenter content is converted into a Flash file (SWF). Your learners will need a web browser (such as Google Chrome or Mozilla Firefox) with the free Adobe Flash Player plug-in enabled, to access and consume the SWF content from your web server or LMS, or from Adobe Connect. Since the Adobe Flash Player plug-in is built into most modern browsers and updated automatically, you will most likely find that your learners have no problem accessing your lessons on a computer with a web browser. (Depending upon the hardware used, and/or the security setup, learners may have to enable or allow the Flash content to play via an alert popup.)

For learners using a mobile device, however, you will need to publish your lesson in HTML5. After you publish your lesson as HTML5, and upload the resulting files to a web server, LMS, or Adobe Connect, it can then be accessed with mobile devices.

If you want to publish a single, standalone file that you can email to a learner or post to an FTP server for download, publishing as a PDF is a viable option. To access the lesson PDF, the learner need a computer with at least version 10 of the Adobe Flash Player installed. According to Adobe, many of the world's modern computers have an appropriate version of the Flash Player needed to open your published PDF. Since the Adobe Flash Player is a free download, learners who do not have the correct version of the Flash Player can easily find and download it directly from Adobe's website (**http://get.adobe.com/ flashplayer/**).

9. Publish the Presenter project as a PDF.

❏ from the left side of the Publish Presentations dialog box, select **Adobe PDF**

As mentioned above, the PDF option produces a single, standalone file that will not rely on a web browser, LMS, or web server. Learners who attempt to open the PDF will need two free programs on their computer: Adobe Reader and Adobe Flash Player. As with the Adobe Flash Player, the Adobe Reader software is also installed on most computers (and is easily downloaded from Adobe's website).

❏ from the **Publish as Adobe PDF** area, click the **Choose** button

❏ open the **Presenter11Data** folder

❏ open the **PublishedLessons** folder

❏ name the PDF **AquoSafetyDemo**

❏ click the **Save** button

❏ at the lower right of the dialog box, ensure **View output after publishing** is selected

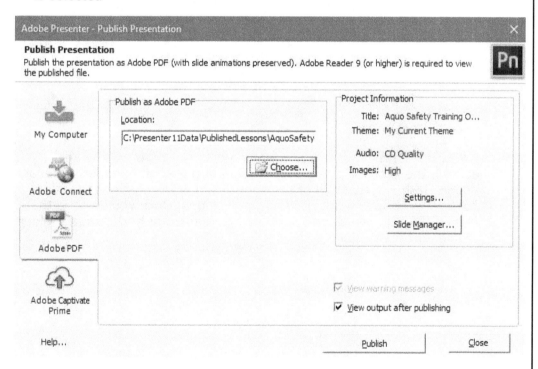

❏ click the **Publish** button

Note: The publishing process can take several minutes to complete

Adobe Presenter will first convert the lesson to a SWF. Once that process is complete, the SWF will automatically be converted into a PDF. Depending on the software installed on your computer, the published PDF will then open in either Adobe Acrobat or Adobe Reader. (Acrobat Pro 2017 is shown below.)

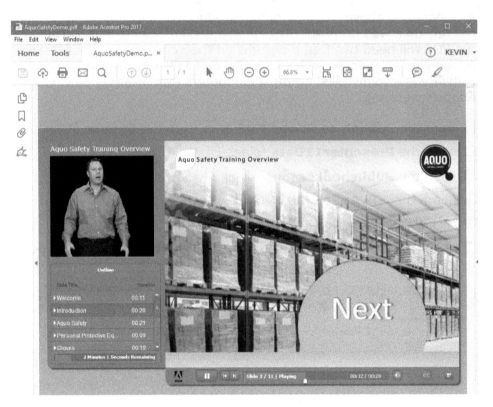

Note: If the lesson does not open and play (as shown in the image above), the likely culprit is your version of the Adobe Reader, Acrobat, Adobe Flash Player, or all of the above. You will likely need to visit Adobe's website and update your applications. Once you've done that, reopen the PDF (which you published to the **PublishedLessons** folder of **Presenter11Data**).

Publishing Confidence Check

1. Close the PDF and return to PowerPoint.

2. Reopen the Presenter **Publish Presentation** dialog box.

3. Select **My Computer** from the list of options at the left of the dialog box.

4. Use the **Choose** button and open the **Presenter11Data** folder.

5. Open the **PublishedLessons** folder.

6. From the **Publish Format** area, select **Both**.

Publishing in Presenter takes your PowerPoint presentation and outputs it into a format that can be consumed (viewed) by the learner via a desktop or laptop computer. Currently, the most common way to publish a Presenter project is as a Flash SWF, an excellent solution because SWF files can be used by the vast majority of the world's personal computers, browsers, and operating systems. Your learners do not need PowerPoint or Presenter installed on their computer to use a SWF, but they do need a modern web browser and the free Adobe Flash Player (www.adobe.com). According to Adobe, the Flash Player is installed on the majority of the world's computers.

SWFs are awesome, but they have a problem. Learners using a device that does not support SWFs, such as the iPad, iPod, and iPhone (that's millions of potential learners), cannot open or view SWF content. Learners using a non-SWF device who attempt to access a web page containing SWFs are typically met with a warning that SWFs are not supported. If you'd like to create content for the non-SWF devices, publish your content as HTML5. Lessons published as HTML5 play on any computers or mobile devices that support HTML5, including the Apple mobile devices.

Because older browsers and computers don't support HTML5, and newer devices and gadgets often don't support SWFs, your safest bet is to select Both. Users who access your content with devices that don't support SWF will be served the HTML5 version of your content; devices that support SWF will be served the SWF version of the published content.

7. From the lower right of the dialog box, ensure **View warning messages** and **View output after publishing** are both selected.

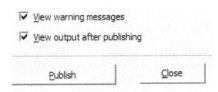

With **View output after publishing** selected, the published output will automatically open in your default web browser. If there are problems with your published content (perhaps there is something in the presentation that contains a SWF and therefore won't work with HTML5 output), the **View warning messages** option will create a tab in the browser itemizing any problem areas.

8. Click the **Publish** button.

The published lesson opens in your default web browser. Feel free to go through the lesson. While this is the same lesson you previewed earlier from within Presenter, this is either the Flash or HTML5 content that will be seen by your learner when this content is accessed online.

Note: If your browser window is blank, try copying the text that appears in the browser address bar and pasting it into the address bar of another browser. We had the best viewing experience using Mozilla Firefox. When accessing content over the web, any browser will work, but Firefox tends to work best when testing locally. Also, you might see the message below. (If so, you can click OK.) Lastly, we've uploaded the content to our web server and you can try viewing it from there: **http://iconlogic.com/elearning/presenter11/index.htm**.

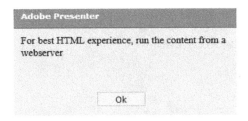

9. When finished previewing, close the web browser.

10. **Minimize** PowerPoint and open the **Presenter11Data** folder.

11. Open the **PublishedLessons** folder.

    All of the contents within the PublishedLessons folder (excluding the PDF) need to be uploaded to a web server and *always kept together*. Never delete or rename any of the published files or folders (doing so will likely break the dependent links between the assets.) The only exception to the renaming rule is index.htm. While it is not typically renamed, you can manually rename it if needed.

data	2/1/18 4:08 PM
metadata	2/1/18 4:08 PM
AquoSafetyDemo.pdf	2/1/18 3:38 PM
as2-wrapper.swf	9/27/12 1:19 PM
breeze-manifest.xml	2/1/18 4:08 PM
browsersniff.js	3/13/12 7:03 AM
components.swf	9/27/12 1:19 PM
index.htm	2/1/18 4:08 PM
SCORM_utilities.js	3/26/14 1:40 PM
standard.js	3/13/12 11:15 AM
Utilities.js	3/13/12 7:03 AM
viewer.swf	8/16/17 11:28 AM
webObject.js	4/28/15 4:44 PM

Speaking of **index.htm**, it's the lesson's **start page** (the page your learners will need to open with a web browser to gain access to the entire lesson). Unless you rename the index file after publishing, index.htm will always be the name of the start page. It's likely that your webmaster or IT professional will want to know the name of the start page should you hand off the published assets to a third party.

12. Close all windows, return to PowerPoint, and then close the AquoSafetyDemo presentation. (There is no need to save the presentation if prompted.)

Characters

Finding quality, royalty-free photographs is always a challenge, especially if you're looking for people that you can use throughout your Presenter projects as guides. Fortunately, Presenter comes with a wonderful assortment of Characters. There are four Character categories (Business, Casual, Illustrated, and Medicine). Most of the categories contain multiple models and poses.

Student Activity: Insert and Resize a Character

1. Using Microsoft PowerPoint, open **CharacterMe** from the Presenter11Data folder.

2. Insert a Character onto slide 2.

   ❑ go to slide **2**

   ❑ on the Ribbon, click the **Adobe Presenter** tab

   ❑ from the **Insert** group, click **Character**

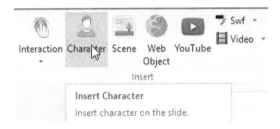

The Characters dialog box opens.

   ❑ at the top left, notice that there is a drop-down menu

   ❑ ensure that **Business** is selected

   ❑ in the left column, scroll down until you see the character named **Samantha**

   ❑ at the right, select any pose that you think looks welcoming

   ❑ click the **OK** button

The photo of Samantha appears on the right side of the slide.

3. Resize an image.

❐ still working on slide 2, **right-click** Samantha and choose **Size and Position**

The Format panel appears at the right of the PowerPoint window.

❐ change the **Scale height** to **57** and then press [**enter**]

Because **Lock aspect ratio** is selected by default, notice that the **Scale width** of the image automatically changes to **57**.

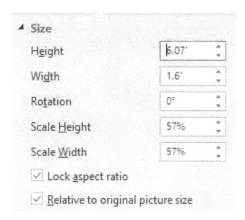

4. Reposition the image.

❐ drag Samantha to the left side of the slide until your slide is similar to the image below

Characters Confidence Check

1. Go to slide 3 and add another version of the Samantha character.

2. Resize and position the character at the left of the slide, similar to the positioning shown below.

3. Go to slide 6 and add a picture of Samantha facing left.

4. Position the new character between the word **me** and the word **myself**.

5. Still working on slide 6, copy and paste the left-facing character to get a second copy.

6. Position the copied character directly on top of the original.

7. On the **Format** tab of the PowerPoint Ribbon, click the **Rotate** drop-down menu and choose **Flip Horizontal**.

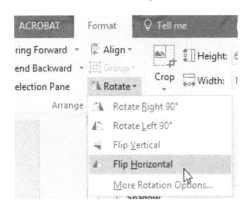

8. Position the two characters similar to the image below.

9. Save your work.

10. Close the presentation.

    You may be wondering why you just placed two copies of a character right on top of each other. By itself, this slide looks a little silly. But with a little PowerPoint Animation magic, you can create an interesting effect.

11. Open **Slide6Animation.pptx**, from the Presenter11Data folder and preview the presentation. You'll see a series of PowerPoint animations, making the character spin from *me* to *myself*.

12. Close the presentation.

Scenes

Scenes are helpful when you're trying to quickly create an eLearning course but you don't have the time to create the background elements to support the slides. To use Presenter's Scenes, you can begin with something as simple as a brand new PowerPoint presentation. Then, from the Adobe Presenter tab, Insert group, you simply click the Scene tool.

On the Insert Scene dialog box, you can select from three different Scenes: Medical, Office-Inside, and Office-Outside. Within each of the categories, there are both sketches and photographs you can use as your Scene.

Student Activity: Create a Scene

1. Create a new, blank PowerPoint presentation.

2. Insert a Medical Scene.

   ❐ from the **Adobe Presenter** tab, **Insert** group, click **Scene**

   The Insert Scene dialog box opens.

   ❐ from the list at the left, select the **Medical** category
   ❐ scroll down and select any one of the photographs

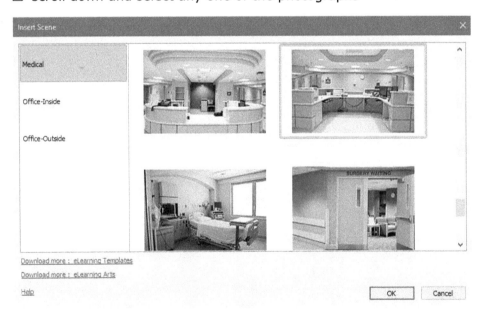

   ❐ click the **OK** button

The selected Scene will be added to your PowerPoint slide and automatically sized to fit perfectly on the slide.

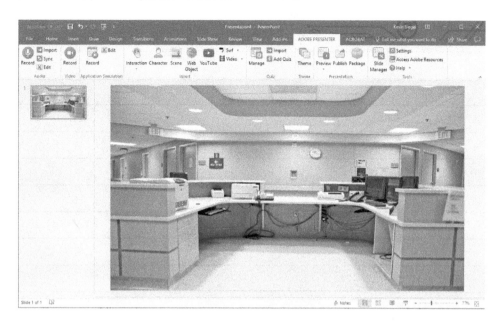

Characters Confidence Check

1. Insert a Character from the Medicine category onto the Scene. (You learned about Characters on page 30.)

2. Resize and reposition the Character as appropriate to work best with your Scene.

3. Add a few new slides to the presentation and then spend a few moments adding more Scenes and Characters.

4. When finished, save the presentation to the Presenter11Data folder as **MyScenes** and then you can close the presentation.

Notes

iCONLOGiC
"Skills and Drills" Learning

Module 2: Audio

In This Module You Will Learn About:

- Voiceover Scripts, page 38
- Recording Voiceover Audio, page 41
- Importing Audio, page 44
- Editing Audio, page 47

And You Will Learn To:

- Add Slides Notes, page 38
- Record Voiceover Audio, page 41
- Import and Review an Audio File, page 44
- Add Silence and Delete Audio, page 47
- Control Audio Volume, page 50

Voiceover Scripts

Scripts and Storyboards were discussed beginning on page 10. Both are critical to creating successful eLearning lessons. It's no surprise that eLearning developers take great care when creating scripts or storyboards. But voiceover scripts often receive a fraction of the time and effort. It's a shame because, simply put, without a voiceover script, you don't have any audio. We've come across more than our fair share of poor voiceover audio. In almost every instance, the poor audio quality wasn't the fault of the voiceover talent or the person who edited the audio. Instead, the culprit was almost always a poorly written voiceover script (or no script at all).

In the lessons that follow, you'll learn how to add a voiceover script to PowerPoint's Notes panel. Since you can record audio directly from within Presenter, you'll also learn how to use the Notes as an aid to recording audio.

Student Activity: Add Slides Notes

1. Using PowerPoint open the **VoiceoverScriptMe.pptx** file from the Presenter11Data folder.

2. Type voiceover text within PowerPoint's Notes pane.

   ❒ ensure you are working on slide **1** and in **Normal** view

   ❒ below the slide, click on the text that says **Click to add notes**

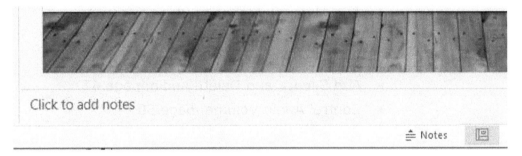

The placeholder text disappears and you can now type your own text.

   ❒ type **This is a Grammar Guide presentation.**

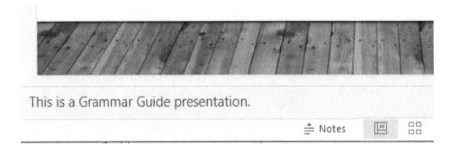

3. Type more voiceover text within PowerPoint's Notes pane.

   ❐ select slide **2**

   ❐ click within the Notes pane and type **Hi, I'm Samantha. Welcome to the Grammar Guide. Today's topic is Me, Myself, and I. Wait. That sounded a little self-centered. I mean our topic is how to tell when to use each of these personal pronouns.**

   Hi, I'm Samantha. Welcome to the Grammar Guide. Today's topic is Me, Myself, and I. Wait. That sounded a little self-centered. I mean our topic is how to tell when to use each of these personal pronouns.

4. Copy and paste voiceover text into PowerPoint's Notes pane.

   ❐ minimize PowerPoint

   ❐ using Microsoft Word, open **VoiceoverTextForSlides.docx** from the Presenter11Data folder.

   ❐ select the text for slide **3**, not including the heading that says Slide 3

   Slide 2

   Hi, I'm Samantha. Welcome to Grammar Guide. Today's topic is Me, Myself, and I. Wait. That sounded a little self-centered. I mean our topic is how to tell when to use each of these personal pronouns.

   Slide 3

   There are times when the word **myself** has grated on my ear—and I have not known why. The misuse of the pronoun **myself** in certain sentences was one of those things that I knew sounded wrong, but I could not quite explain why.

   ❐ press [**ctrl**] [**c**] to copy the selected text to the clipboard

   ❐ return to PowerPoint (the **VoiceoverScriptMe** presentation should still be open)

   ❐ select slide **3**

   ❐ click within the Notes pane

   ❐ press [**ctrl**] [**v**] to paste the voiceover text into the Notes pane

   There are times when someone's grammar has grated on my ear—and I have not known why. The misuse of the pronoun **myself** in certain sentences was one of those things that I knew sounded wrong, but I could not quite explain why.

5. Save your work.

Voiceover Confidence Check

1. Copy and paste the voiceover text from the Word document to the Notes pane for slides 4, 5, and 6.

   Each slide should now contain voiceover text in their respective Notes pane.

2. Save and close **VoiceoverScriptMe**.

3. Close the Word document (there is no need to save the document if prompted).

Recording Voiceover Audio

Adobe Presenter allows you to record voiceover for each slide—or for a series of slides. You can even synchronize your voiceover with animations on the slide to simulate what you would do in a live classroom. If you prefer, you can record the voiceover separately, by using a sound-recording program such as Adobe Audition, or hire voiceover talent to do the recording.

If you plan to record your own audio, you first need a microphone connected to your computer. Once you've got the microphone, consider the following:

Setup: If you plan to use high-end audio hardware, such as a mixer or preamplifier, plug your microphone into the hardware and then plug the hardware into your computer's "line in" port. Set the volume on your mixer or preamplifier to just under zero (this will minimize distortion).

Microphone placement: The microphone should be positioned four to six inches from your mouth to reduce the chance that nearby sounds are recorded. Ideally, you should position the microphone above your nose and pointed down at your mouth. Also, if you position the microphone just to the side of your mouth, you can soften the sound of the letters *S* and *P*.

Microphone technique: It's a good idea to keep a glass of water close by and, just before recording, take a drink. To eliminate the annoying breathing and lip smack sounds, turn away from the microphone, take a deep breath, exhale, take another deep breath, open your mouth, turn back toward the microphone and start speaking. Speak slowly. When recording for the first time, many people race through the content. Take your time.

Student Activity: Record Voiceover Audio

1. Open the **RecordAudioMe.pptx** file from the Presenter11Data folder.

   This presentation contains several slides. Each slide contains voiceover text with the Notes pane.

2. Record a voiceover for slide 1.

   ❏ select slide **1**

   ❏ from the **Adobe Presenter** tab, **Audio** section, click **Record**

   A dialog box opens that allows you to calibrate your microphone.

   ❏ read aloud the sentence displayed in the dialog box repeatedly until you see the green **Input Level OK** message

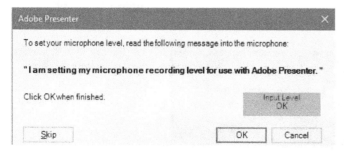

   ❏ click the **OK** button

PowerPoint goes into slideshow view, and the Recording dialog box opens.

❑ in the upper right of the dialog box, click the **Show script** tool

The Script you added to the Notes pane opens in its own window.

3. Enlarge the font size for the Script text.

❑ in the lower left of the Script window, click the **Increase Font Size** tool

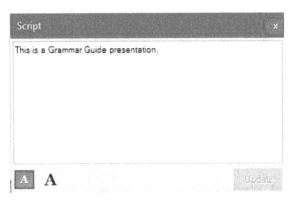

4. Record audio for the first slide.

❑ in the Recording dialog box, click the **Record audio** tool

❑ read aloud the text displayed within the Script window

❑ click the **Stop recording** tool (just to the right of the Recording audio tool)

Now that you have recorded audio, the Recording dialog box updates to display a Play tool (the white triangle), a Save tool, and a Discard tool.

❑ click the **Play** tool

You'll hear your recorded audio on the first slide and then automatically be taken to the second slide, where you could record more audio. If you are unhappy with the recording, you can click the **Previous** slide tool (shown being clicked in the image below), click the **Discard** tool, and re-record the audio.

5. If you are satisfied with the recorded audio for slide 1, click the **Save** tool. (Otherwise, go back to slide 1 and re-record.)

6. Close the Recording dialog box.

7. Record audio for the second slide.

   ❑ select slide **2**

   ❑ from the **Adobe Presenter** tab, **Audio** section, click the **Record** tool

   Once again, a dialog box opens that will allow you to calibrate your microphone.

   ❑ read aloud the sentence displayed in the dialog box repeatedly until you see the green **Input Level OK** message

   ❑ click the **OK** button

   The Recording dialog box opens again.

   ❑ click the **Show script** tool

8. Enlarge the font size for the Script text.

   ❑ click the **Increase Font Size** tool

9. Record audio for the slide.

   ❑ in the Recording dialog box, click the **Record audio** tool

   ❑ read aloud the text displayed within the Script window

   ❑ click the **Stop recording** tool

   ❑ click the **Play** tool

10. If you are satisfied with the recorded audio, click the **Save** tool and then close the Recording dialog box.

11. Save and close the presentation.

Importing Audio

You can import two types of audio files into a Presenter project: WAV and MP3. You can add audio to just about anything. During the activity that follows, you will import audio to some rollover captions and rollover images.

WAV (WAVE): WAV files are one of the original digital audio standards. These kind of files, although of high quality, can be very large. In fact, typical WAV audio files can easily take up to *several megabytes of storage per minute* of playing time. If your learner has a slow Internet connection, the download times for large files is unacceptable.

MP3 (MPEG Audio Layer III): MP3 files are compressed digital audio files. File sizes in this format are typically 90 percent smaller than WAV files.

> **Note:** You can learn more about digital audio formats by visiting **www.webopedia.com/DidYouKnow/Computer_Science/2005/ digital_audio_formats.asp** (a site that details common audio formats).

Student Activity: Import and Review an Audio File

1. Open **ImportAudioMe.pptx** from the Presenter11Data folder.

   This project contains 16 slides. Each of the slides contains slide notes but no audio.

2. Import audio for one slide.

   ❏ from the Adobe Presenter tab, **Audio** group, click the **Import** tool

   The **Import Audio** dialog box opens.

   ❏ select **Slide 1** and then click the **Browse** button

   The Select File(s) to Import dialog box opens.

   ❏ navigate to the **Presenter11Data** folder

   ❏ open the **Audio** folder

   ❏ open **slide1.wav**

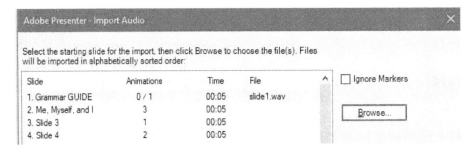

❑ on the **Import Audio** dialog box, click the **OK** button

When the import process is complete, the **Import complete** alert appears.

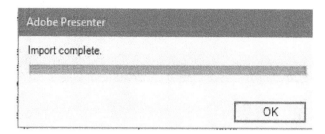

❑ click the **OK** button

3. Use the Audio Edit tool to review audio.

❑ from the Adobe Presenter tab, **Audio** group, click the **Edit** tool

The Edit Audio dialog box opens. At the far left you can see blue, squiggly lines. The lines are known as a **waveform**, which is the digital representative for the audio file you just imported onto slide 1. You'll listen to the audio next.

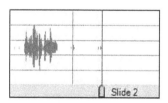

❑ at the lower left of the Edit Audio dialog box, locate the **Play** tool

This same button will become the Pause button during playback.

❑ click the **Play** tool

A black line—the Playhead—progresses across the waveform, and you hear the voiceover audio that you imported. If you listen carefully, you can also hear some extra noises (almost a clap sound and then a mouse click). You'll learn to remove these kinds of noises soon. Since there isn't any audio after the mouse click sound, allowing the Playhead to continue to move doesn't make much sense so it's time to Pause the playback.

❏ click the **Pause** button

❏ click the **Close** button to close the Edit Audio dialog box

4. Save the project.

Importing Audio Confidence Check

1. Still working within the ImportAudioMe project, import **slide2.wav** onto slide 2.

2. Import **slide3.wav** onto slide 3.

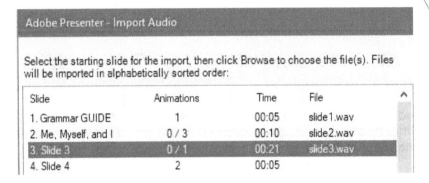

3. Using the **Edit** tool on the Audio group, **Play** the audio that you've just imported.

   You'll notice that there are plenty of noises between the waves on the waveform that need to be cleaned up. You'll take care of that next.

4. Save and close the project.

Editing Audio

In a perfect world, audio that you record or import would be perfect. There wouldn't be noises between the waves of a waveform. There wouldn't be any narrator gaffes to delete and the audio levels from one waveform to the next would be consistent. Unfortunately, the world's not perfect and knowing how to make simple edits to an audio file is a necessity. While Presenter isn't the most powerful audio editing tool in the world, you'll find that there are enough features to allow you to delete unwanted parts of a waveform, add silence, and even control the volume levels across an entire presentation.

Student Activity: Add Silence and Delete Audio

1. Open the **EditAudioMe.pptx** file from the Presenter11Data folder.

   This 16-slide presentation is loaded with audio. Much of it needs editing.

   ❑ from the Adobe Presenter tab, **Audio** group, click the **Edit** tool

   The Edit Audio dialog box opens.

   ❑ if necessary, click at the far left edge of the waveform to move the Playhead to the beginning of the waveform

2. Zoom closer to the waveform.

   ❑ at the far right of the Edit Audio dialog box, drag the Zoom slider **right** to zoom a bit closer to the waveform

   ❑ at the bottom left of the dialog box, click the **Play** tool and listen to the audio on the first couple of slides

   On slide 1, a sound occurs after the narrator is finished speaking. (The problem area is shown circled below.)

3. Replace unwanted audio with silence.

❏ select the area of the waveform shown below (it's about 2 seconds of audio)

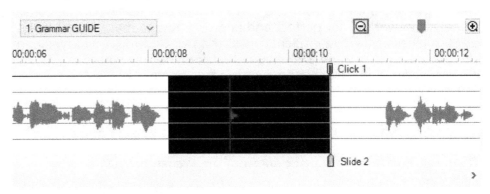

❏ at the top of the Edit Audio dialog box, click the **Insert Silence** tool

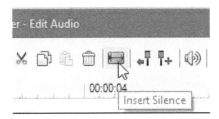

The Insert Silence dialog box reopens.

❏ replace the **Insert** value with **1** second

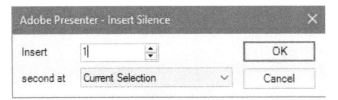

❏ click the **OK** button

Even though you selected more than one second on the waveform, the noise was replaced with a single second of silence.

4. Review the edits.

❏ click at the far left edge of the waveform to move the Playhead to the beginning of the waveform

❏ click the **Play** tool and listen to the audio on the first slide

The problematic sounds should have been removed.

❏ **Pause** the playback, click the **Save** button; then click the **Close** button

5. Delete an audio segment.

   ❏ from the Adobe Presenter tab, **Audio** group, click the **Edit** tool

   ❏ click at the beginning of the audio for slide **2** and then click the **Play** tool

   As the Playhead reaches the end of slide 2, notice that there is a sharp smacking sound. You have learned that you can replace selected audio segments with silence. However, if you use that technique, you also have to worry about how much silence to use in place of the sound. In this case, it's a bit quicker to simply select and delete the sound.

   ❏ click the **Pause** tool and then, on the waveform, select the sound near the end of slide 2

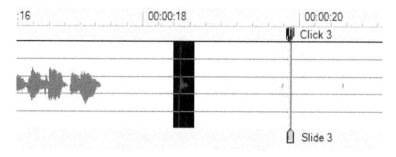

   ❏ at the top of the Edit Audio dialog box, click the **Delete** tool

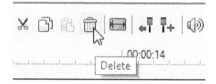

   The selected segment of the waveform is gone.

   ❏ click the **Save** button and then click the **Close** button

Student Activity: Control Audio Volume

1. Ensure that the **EditAudioMe** project is still open.

2. Lower the volume of audio.

   ❏ from the Adobe Presenter tab, **Audio** group, click the **Edit** tool

   ❏ scroll to the right and click the audio for slide **5**

   ❏ click the **Play** tool

   The audio level for the presentation sounds perfectly fine. However, when you get to slide 6, you'll notice that the volume for the audio on slide 6 is much louder than the audio on slide 5. You'll attempt to fix the problem by lowering the volume on slide 6.

   ❏ click the **Pause** tool

   ❏ select and then double-click the waveform for slide **6**

   Double-clicking the waveform is a quick way to highlight the audio for the slide.

   ❏ at the top of the Edit Audio dialog box, click the **Adjust volume** tool

   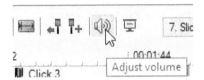

   The Adjust Volume dialog box opens.

   ❏ at the left of the dialog box drag the Volume slide **down** to **50%**

   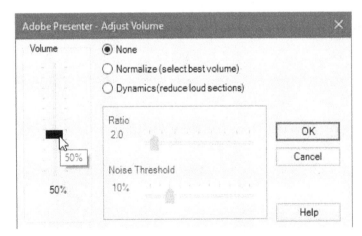

   ❏ click the **OK** button

   Because you lowered the volume for the slide 6 audio, the height of the waveform for slide 6 has gotten shorter. Generally speaking, the shorter a waveform, the lower its volume. While the waveform for slide 6 is still a bit taller than the waveform for slide 5, the difference in the volume between the two slides has been minimized.

Audio Editing Confidence Check

1. Spend the next few moments raising or lowering the volume of the audio throughout the presentation until the levels sound consistent to you.

2. Listen to the audio and either insert Silence or delete unwanted segments of audio as necessary.

3. Save and close the presentation.

Notes

iCONLOGiC
"Skills and Drills" Learning

Module 3: Video and Pictures

In This Module You Will Learn About:

- Slide Video, page 54
- Sidebar Video, page 59
- Pictures, page 61

And You Will Learn To:

- Add a Video to a Slide, page 54
- Edit an Imported Video, page 57
- Import a Sidebar Video, page 59
- Import a Picture Onto a Slide, page 61

Slide Video

Presenter supports several types of video formats including Windows media files (afs, wmv, and mpg), Quick Time files (mp4, dv, dvi, mov, and 3g), and Flash Video (flv). If your computer setup includes a video camera, you can also record your own video. When adding videos to a presentation, you can elect to import the video directly to a slide or have the video appear on the Sidebar. You'll learn both techniques during this module.

Student Activity: Add a Video to a Slide

1. Using PowerPoint, open the **AquoSafetyDemo.pptx** file from the **Presenter11Data** folder.

   This presentation contains several videos and images. You'll be adding these videos into a different project soon. Before learning how, it will be helpful to preview the entire presentation and review the images that are being used and explore the videos.

2. Preview the presentation.

   ❏ at the right side of the **Adobe Presenter** tab, click the **Preview** drop-down menu and choose **Preview Presentation**

   There is a large video on the first slide. You'll be adding this video and removing some of the original content. As the second slide appears, there's a video guide in the upper left of the screen introducing the lesson. And then, as the lesson moves forward, there are images and videos on several slides.

3. Close the preview.

4. Close the AquoSafetyDemo presentation.

5. Using PowerPoint, open the **VideoImageMe.pptx** file from the Presenter11Data folder.

   This is the same presentation as **AquoSafetyDemo**, except it's missing the videos and the images.

6. Insert a video onto slide 1.

   ❏ select slide **1** (if necessary)

   ❏ from the **Adobe Presenter** tab, **Insert** group, click the **Video** tool

The **Import Video** dialog box opens

❑ navigate to the **Presenter11Data** folder

❑ open the **Images_Videos** folder

❑ select (but don't open) **welcomeToLesson.mp4**

❑ at the bottom right of the dialog box, click the **Import On** drop-down menu and select **Slide 1** (if necessary)

❑ from the **As** area, ensure **Slide Video** is selected

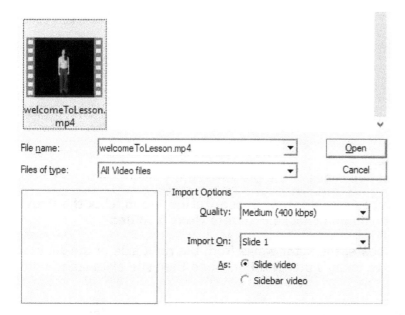

❑ at the very bottom of the dialog box, select the **Preview** check box

You will likely receive a message that QuickTime, Apple's multimedia technology, is needed to import the MP4 videos. If you are able to install QuickTime on your computer, we suggest that you do so. If you are unable to install QuickTime, click the **Cancel** button and import the F4V videos included in the **F4V_Videos** folder for the activities in this module.

A preview of the video plays within the preview window.

❑ once the preview is finished, click the **Open** button

The video will be inserted in the middle of slide 1.

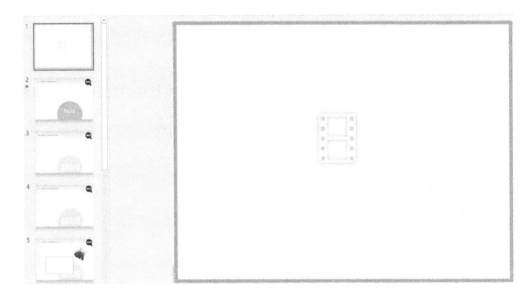

7. Preview the first five slides of the presentation.

   ❑ from the Adobe Presenter tab, **Presentation** group, click the **Preview** drop-down menu and choose **Preview Next 5 Slides**

   After slide 1 appears, the actor walks from the right side of the slide, turns, says "Welcome to today's presentation," and then she exits stage right. How cool is that?

   ❑ click the **Rewind** tool on the playbar and watch the video again

   Notice that there is a problem at the end of the video. If you listen carefully, you can hear the video director say "Cut" just before the video ends. You'll learn during the next activity that you can easily delete a portion of the video without leaving Presenter.

   ❑ close the preview window

8. Save your work.

Student Activity: Edit an Imported Video

1. Ensure that the **VideoImageMe.pptx** file is still open.

2. Open the Video Editor.

   ❑ select slide **1**

   ❑ from the Adobe Presenter tab, **Insert** group, click the **Video** drop-down menu and choose **Edit**

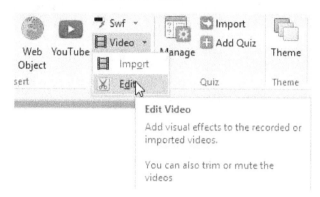

   The **Edit Video** dialog box opens and the video plays automatically (and continuously).

3. Delete a portion of a video.

   ❑ just below the video, click the **Pause** button

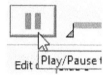

   The video immediately stops playing and the Pause button becomes a **Play** button.

   ❑ click the **Play** button to allow the video to resume playing

   As the video plays, and then replays, notice that there is a black, upside down triangle that tracks across the playbar. The triangle marks time along the playbar.

   As the triangle approaches the 10-second mark, you'll be able to hear someone say "cut." You'll need to remove that segment from the video.

   ❑ click the **Pause** button

   ❑ at the far right of the playbar, locate the gray marker that's just to the left of the Trashcan icon

❏ drag the marker (shown circled below) **left** until it lines up with the 10-second mark

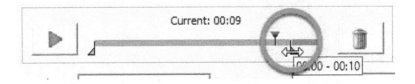

Anything to the right of the marker will be hidden and will not appear when your preview or publish the presentation.

❏ click the **Play** button to allow the video to resume playing

When the triangle reaches the marker, the video will rewind and ignore the remaining part of the video.

Note: You have not cropped or changed the video in any way. You have simply hidden part of the video from the learner. If you change your mind or simply need to show all of the video, all you would need to do is drag the marker back to its original position.

❏ click the **OK** button

4. Preview the first five slides of the presentation.

As the video plays again, notice this time that the audio gaffe at the end of the video has been removed.

5. Close the preview window and then save your work.

Videos Confidence Check

1. Still working within the **VideoImageMe** presentation, import the **gloves.mp4** video onto slide **5** as Slide Video.

2. Drag and position the video to the middle of the green box on the slide.

3. Preview the Next 5 slides to see the newest video you've added to the presentation.

4. Close the preview and then import the **shirt.mp4** video onto slide **6** as Slide Video.

5. Import the **hardhat.mp4** video onto slide **7** as Slide Video.

6. Import the **boots.mp4** video onto slide **8** as Slide Video.

7. Import the **goggles.mp4** video onto slide **9** as Slide Video.

8. Resize the videos if necessary to fit within their respective boxes.

9. Go back to slide 5 and preview the Next 5 slides to see the videos you've added to slides 5 through 9.

10. Save your work.

Sidebar Video

So far you've learned how to import and edit slide video. But you can also import a video and have it appear in a Sidebar (a navigation area you can include on either side of your Presenter eLearning lesson). Sidebar videos are perfect for showing video guides/presenters or avatars along with a TOC for the presentation. In the activity that follows, you'll add a message from a manager who will explain the value of the lesson that the learner is about to watch.

Student Activity: Import a Sidebar Video

1. Ensure that the **VideoImageMe.pptx** is still open.

2. Import a video and use it in the Sidebar.

   ❏ select slide **2**

   ❏ from the Adobe Presenter tab, **Insert** group, click the **Video** tool

   ❏ from **Presenter11Data** folder, open the **Images_Videos** folder

   ❏ select (but don't open) **Safety_Intro.mp4**

   ❏ at the bottom right of the dialog box, click the **Import On** drop-down menu and select **Slide 2**

   ❏ from the **As** area, select **Sidebar video**

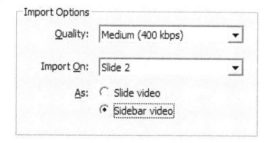

   ❏ click the **Open** button

   While you might have expected the video to appear on the slide, there's nothing there. The video has been assigned to the Sidebar which you'll learn about next.

3. Show the Sidebar.

   ❏ from the Adobe Presenter tab, **Theme** group, click the **Theme** tool

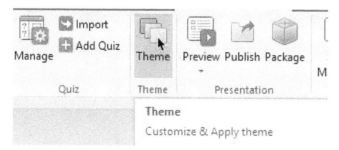

The Theme Editor opens. This dialog box allows you to enable a Sidebar, display the Presenter's information, enable Panes and more. You'll visit this dialog box multiple times over the course of this book. For now, you're only looking to enable the Sidebar.

❏ from the **Customize** area at the right, select **Show Sidebar**

❏ from the **Location** drop-down menu, ensure **Left** is selected

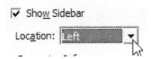

❏ click the **OK** button

4. Starting on slide 2, preview the Next 5 slides to see both the Sidebar and the Sidebar video (indicated by the arrow in the image below).

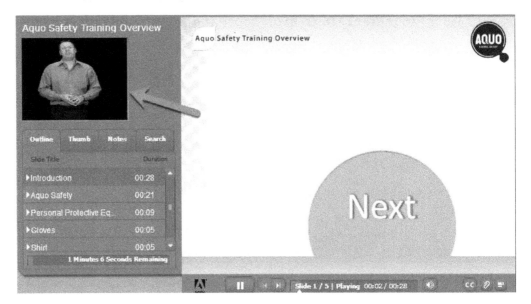

5. Close the preview window.

6. Save your work.

Pictures

You can import several graphic formats onto a PowerPoint slide including, but not limited to, BMPs (Windows Bitmap), GIFs (Graphics Interchange Format), JPG or JPEG (Joint Photographic Expert Group), WMFs (MetaFiles), and PNGs (Portable Network Graphics).

Once the image has been imported onto a slide, it can be manipulated like any PowerPoint image (you can resize images, crop them, group them, animate them, re-color them, etc.).

Student Activity: Import a Picture Onto a Slide

1. Ensure that the **VideoImageMe.pptx** is still open.

2. Add an image to slide 2.

   ❑ select slide **2** and, from the PowerPoint Ribbon, select the **Insert** tab (not the Presenter tab this time)

   ❑ from the **Images** group, and click the **Pictures** tool

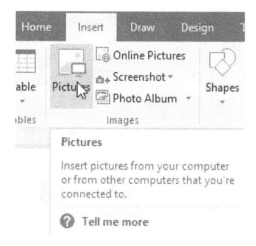

   ❑ from the **Presenter11Data** folder, open the **Images_Videos** folder

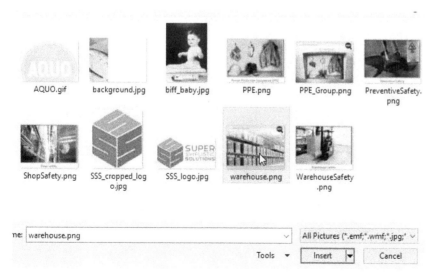

☐ open **warehouse.png**

The image is very large and covers the entire slide.

3. Send the image behind other slide elements.

☐ right-click the middle of the image you just imported and choose
Send to Back

4. Save your work.

Images Confidence Check

1. Still working within the **VideoImageMe.pptx** project, insert the following pictures onto slide **3**:

   PPE.png

   ShopSafety.png

   WarehouseSafety.png

   PreventiveSafety.png

2. Position the four images on the slide similar to the picture shown below.

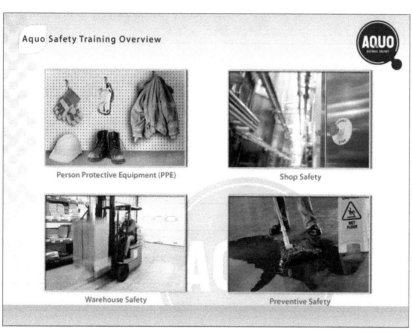

3. Go to slide 4 and insert the **PPE_Group.png** picture in the middle of the slide.

4. Preview the presentation to view both the videos you've imported during this module and the images.

5. Close the preview.

6. Save and close the presentation.

Notes

iCONLOGiC

"Skills and Drills" Learning

Module 4: Interactive eLearning

In This Module You Will Learn About:

- Interactions, page 66
- Scenario Interactions, page 73

And You Will Learn To:

- Insert a Word Search Interaction, page 66
- Manage a Slide, page 71
- Create a Scenario Interaction, page 73
- Create a Hyperlink, page 78

Interactions

Interactions, also referred to as Smart Learning Interactions, are widgets (SWFs) that allow you to quickly insert interactive objects onto a slide. Adobe Presenter comes with a wide range of Interactions such as Process Cycles and Word Search; and you can download more from the Adobe Presenter website. As you work with Interactions, you'll find that you can customize not only the content but also the look and feel of the Interaction.

Student Activity: Insert a Word Search Interaction

1. Using PowerPoint, open the **InteractMe.pptx** file from the **Presenter11Data** folder.

2. Insert the Word Search Interaction on slide 10.

   ❑ select slide **10**

   ❑ from the **Adobe Presenter** tab, **Insert** group, click the **Interaction** drop-down menu and choose **Insert Interaction**

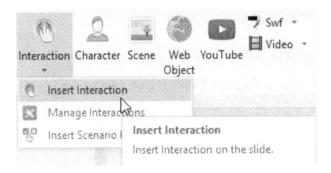

The Insert Interaction dialog box opens.

   ❑ select the **Word Search** interaction

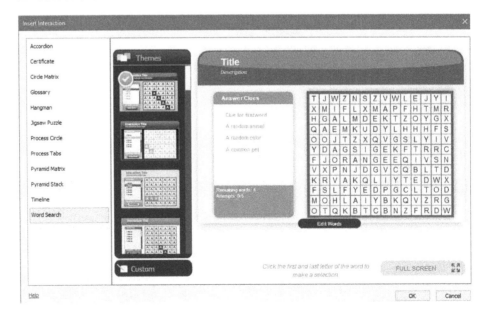

   ❑ click the **OK** button

The Interaction is added to the slide. You will add content to the Interaction next.

3. Add a Title and a Description to an Interaction.

❑ from the Adobe Presenter tab, **Insert** group, click the **Interaction** drop-down menu and choose **Manage Interactions**

The Manage Interactions dialog box opens; the Interaction you added to slide 10 is selected.

❑ click the **Edit** button

The Insert Interaction dialog box reopens. While most dialog boxes only allow you to select options from drop-down menus and click buttons, this dialog box is where you'll actually add content to the Interaction.

❑ double-click the word **Title** and replace it with the phrase **Word Search**

❑ double-click the **Description** and replace it with **Find the Safety Equipment Hidden Among the Letters.**

❑ click the **OK** button

4. Add clues and words to the Word Search Interaction.

☐ from the Adobe Presenter tab, **Insert** group, click the **Interaction** drop-down menu and choose **Manage Interactions**

☐ on the Manage Interactions dialog box, click the **Edit** button

☐ near the **bottom** of the Word Search Interaction, click **Edit Words**

The **WordFind Edit** dialog box opens.

☐ from the **Puzzle Size** area, ensure the first, smaller square is selected

☐ in the first column, change words in the **Question 1** area to **Protects your head**

☐ in the **Answer 1** area, change the word to **HardHat** (no spaces)

Interaction Confidence Check

1. Continue filling in the first two columns (6 words and 6 clues) to match the image below).

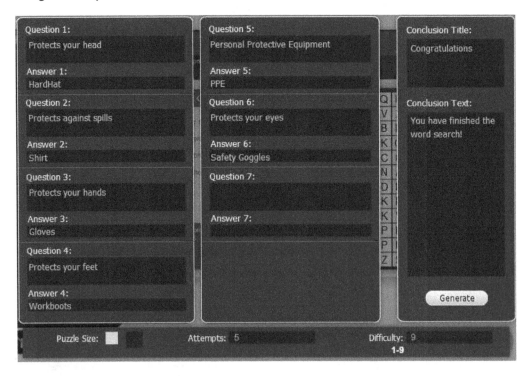

2. When finished, click the **Generate** button (located in the lower right of the dialog box) and then click the **OK** button.

3. Save your work.

4. Open the Interaction for editing again.

5. From the Themes column, scroll down and select the **Theme 15**.
   (Theme names appear when you hover over each Theme.)

6. From the bottom left of the dialog box, click the **Custom** button.

   There are three areas of the Interaction that you can customize: Grid, Answers, and Header. While each of the areas allows you to change multiple attributes, you'll find that some areas of the Interaction cannot be customized.

7. Click **Header** and then click **Color**.

8. Click the **Header background color** swatch (the square containing the color), change the color to **#A0CE5E** and then press [**enter**]

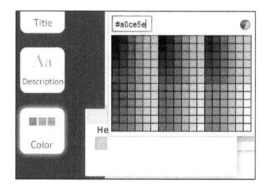

   The **#A0CE5E** value you typed will result in a green accent color that is used on some of the other slides in the lesson.

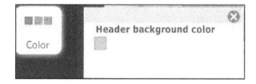

9. Close the **Header background color** dialog box and then click **Title**.

10. Change the Font to **Calibri**, the Style to **Bold** and the Size to **24**.

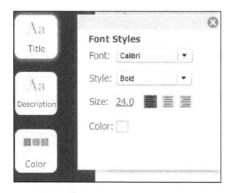

11. Close the Font Styles dialog box and then click **Description**.

12. Change the Font to **Calibri**.

13. Close the Font Styles dialog box.

14. From the left side of the Interaction dialog box, click **Custom**.

15. Spend a few minutes customizing the Grid and Answers.

16. When finished, click the **OK** button.

17. Save your work.

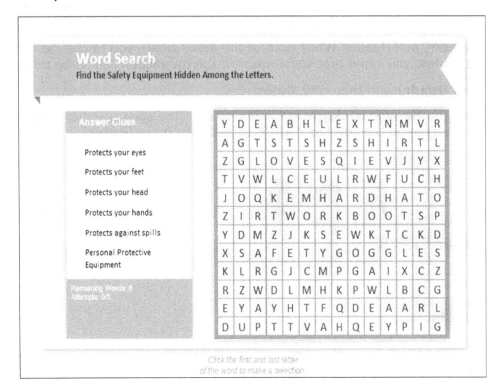

Note: Presenter's Interactions are fun. Unfortunately, we also found them to be resource hogs that frequently cause Presenter to crash. We encourage you to be extra diligent about saving your work, especially when working with Interactions.

Student Activity: Manage a Slide

1. Ensure that the **InteractMe.pptx** presentation is still open.

2. Change how a slide can be advanced by the learner.

   ❏ from the Adobe Presenter tab, **Tools** group, click the **Slide Manager** tool

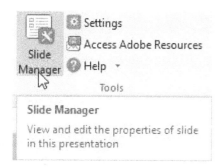

   The Slide Manager dialog box opens.

   ❏ scroll down and select slide **10**

   ❏ change the **Advance by User** option to **No**

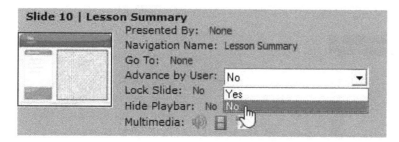

   ❏ click the **OK** button

3. Preview a few slides.

   ❏ select slide **9**

   ❏ from the Adobe Presenter tab, **Presentation** group, click the **Preview** drop-down menu and choose **Preview Next 5 Slides**

   When you get to slide 10, you'll find that you are unable to work with the Interaction at all; instead you'll automatically jump ahead to a quiz. You'll need to go back and edit slide 10 so that it doesn't move forward until the learner clicks the **Play** button on the playbar.

   ❏ close the Preview

4. Change a slide's navigation so that it stops until the learner is ready to advance to the next slide.

   ❏ from the Adobe Presenter tab, **Tools** group, click the **Slide Manager** tool

   The Slide Manager dialog box reopens.

❑ select slide **10** and change the **Advance by User** option back to **Yes**

❑ click the **OK** button

5. Select slide **9** and preview the next 5 slides.

When you get to slide 10 this time, the slide will stop allowing you to play the Word Game. When you are finished with the game, click the Play button on the playbar to continue with the lesson. (This is the Advance by User feature in action.)

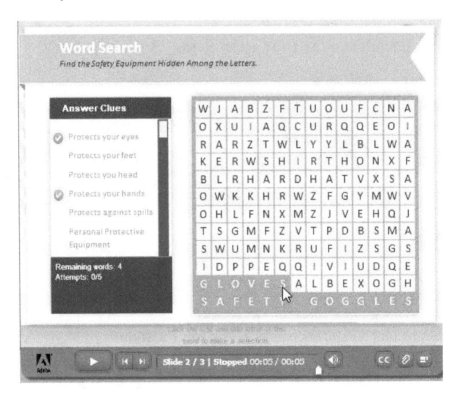

6. Close the Preview.

7. Save and close the presentation.

Scenario Interactions

Scenarios combine the concept of Characters (page 30) and Scenes (page 34), but take both to a new level. When adding a Scenario, you can choose from four categories: Business, Call Center, Generic, and Medical. After you've added the Scenario, you'll notice that several slides are automatically inserted within the presentation, each allowing for learner interactivity via a series of clickable areas. Depending on what the learner decides to click, the Scenario provides a different learner experience.

Student Activity: Create a Scenario Interaction

1. Preview an existing Scenario.

   ❏ using PowerPoint, open the **ScenarioSample.pptx** file from the **Presenter11Data** folder

   ❏ from the Adobe Presenter tab, **Presentation** group, click the **Preview** drop-down menu and choose **Preview Presentation**

   This is the Scenario you will create from scratch in the next few moments. It's a medical scenario asking you to determine the best course of action for a patient.

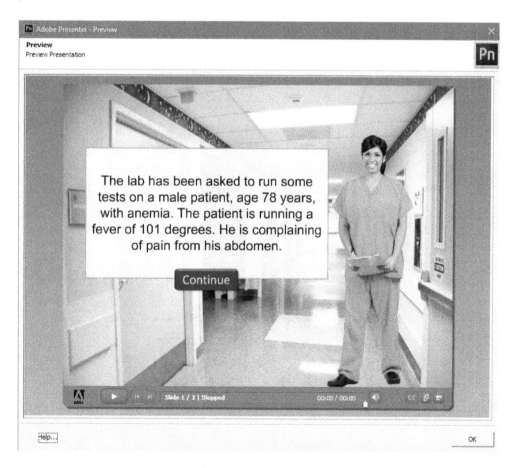

   ❏ click the **Continue** button

   ❏ work through the Scenario, clicking the option that you think is best

2. When finished working through the Scenario, close the Preview window.

3. Close the presentation.

4. Insert a Scenario Interaction.

   ❑ using PowerPoint, open the **ScenarioMe.pptx** file from the **Presenter11Data** folder

   ❑ from the Adobe Presenter tab, **Insert** group, click the **Interaction** drop-down menu and choose **Insert Scenario Interaction**

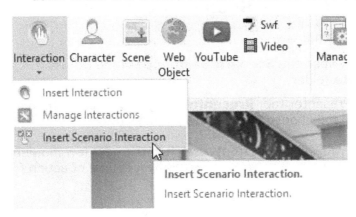

The Insert Scenario Interaction dialog box opens.

   ❑ from the drop-down menu at the top left of the dialog box, choose **Medical**

   ❑ from the bottom of the dialog box, ensure the **Number of Options** is set to **3**

   ❑ from the **Correct Option** drop-down menu, choose **C**

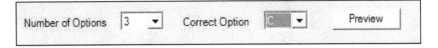

   ❑ click the **OK** button

Six slides are added to the presentation.

5. Reposition a slide.

   ☐ using PowerPoint's **Slide Sorter** at the left, drag slide **1** all the way down so that it is the last slide in the presentation

   The slide containing the "Thanks for working through this..." text should now be the seventh and last slide in the presentation.

6. Add content to a slide.

   ☐ go to slide **1** and replace the existing text with **The lab has been asked to run some tests on a male patient, age 78 years, with anemia. The patient is running a fever of 101 degrees. He is complaining of pain from his abdomen.**

7. Edit the instructions and the options.

   ☐ go to slide **2**

   ☐ select the instruction text and replace it with **Which of these blood tests would you expect to run for this patient?**

   ☐ replace the placeholder text for Option A with **HCG**

   ☐ replace Option B text with **Hematocrit only**

   ☐ replace Option C text with **CBC**

   The first two slides should look similar to this:

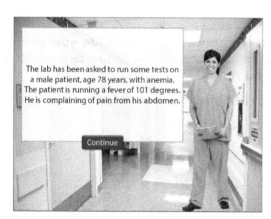 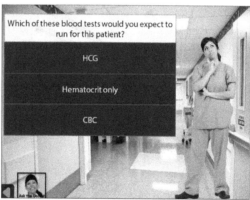

8. Save the presentation.

Scenario Confidence Check

1. Replace the text on slide 3 with **CBC—a Complete Blood Count—is the best answer. This will include counts of the white blood cells, red blood cells, and platelets. It also includes the MCV, hematocrit, MCH, and several other measures.**

2. Format the objects on the slide so that the appearance is similar to the image below.

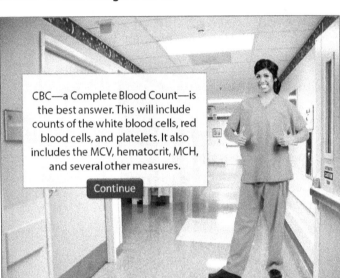

3. Replace the text on slide **4** with **Well, hematocrit will give you some of what you want, but it will not include the white blood cell count and some of the other measures you need.**

4. Format the objects on the slide so that the appearance is similar to the image below.

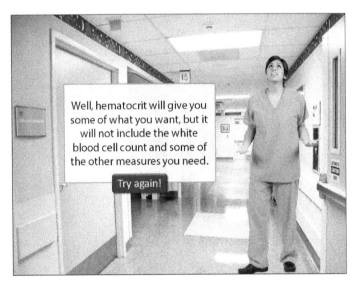

5. Replace the text on slide **5** with **Wait! That can't be it. That would be a pregnancy test!**

6. Format the objects on the slide so that the appearance is similar to the image below.

7. Replace the text on slide **6** with **For a patient with anemia and also abdominal pain, you will want to get counts of the white blood cells as well as several measures of the hemoglobin, including the hematocrit and MCV.**

8. Format the objects on the slide so that the appearance is similar to the image below.

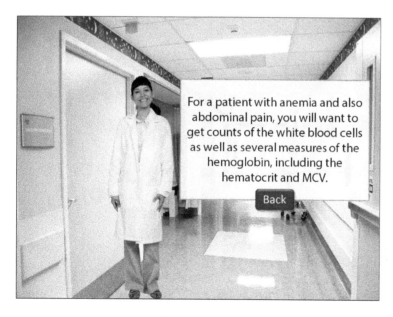

9. Save the presentation.

Student Activity: Create a Hyperlink

1. Ensure that the **ScenarioMe.pptx** presentation is still open.

2. Add a hyperlink to a slide object.

   ❑ on slide **7**, right-click the **Repeat the lesson** button and choose **Link (or Hyperlink)**

   The Insert Hyperlink dialog box opens.

   ❑ from the **Link to** area, select **Place in This Document**

   ❑ from the **Select a place in this document** area, select **1. Scenario Introduction Screen**

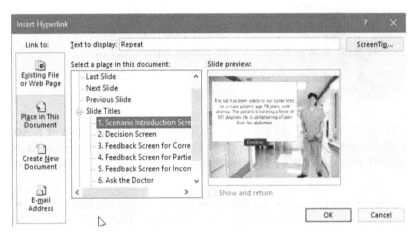

   ❑ click the **OK** button

3. Review an existing hyperlink.

   ❑ select slide **2**, right-click the box containing **CBC** and choose **Edit Link**

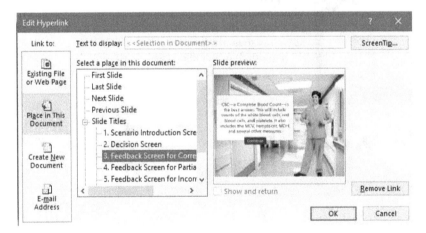

   Notice that the slide object has already been hyperlinked to slide 3 which is the correct answer. This hyperlink, and the other hyperlinks you will find throughout the Scenario, was added automatically when the Scenario Interaction was inserted into the presentation. Since the navigation was added for you, all you had to worry about was adding the content. *How cool is that?*

❏ click the **Cancel** button

Note: You can remove a hyperlink by right-clicking an object and choosing **Remove Link**.

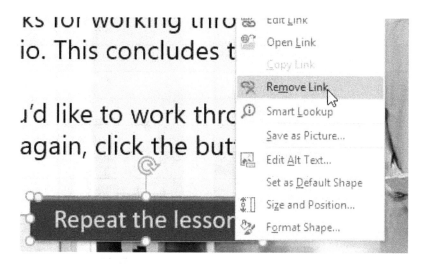

4. Preview the presentation.

5. When finished working through the Scenario, close the Preview window.

6. Save and close the presentation.

Notes

_____

_____

_____

_____

_____

_____

_____

_____

_____

_____

_____

_____

_____

_____

_____

_____

_____

_____

_____

_____

_____

_____

_____

_____

_____

_____

_____

_____

_____

_____

_____

_____

_____

_____

Module 5: Quizzing

In This Module You Will Learn About:

- Creating Quizzes, page 82

And You Will Learn To:

- Add a Quiz, page 82
- Insert a Graded Question, page 86
- Add a Survey Question, page 89

Creating Quizzes

Learning can be exhausting. If you think about it, there's only so much learning that can effectively occur over a set amount of time. As professional trainers, we certainly have the ability to force feed information to our students. However, without regularly-scheduled breaks, the ability of our students to both learn and retain information is minimized. Beyond breaks, we encourage our learners to openly discuss with their classmates (and with us) what they learned during class. We've found that the simple act of discussing the concepts taught in class greatly improves the students' experience, enhances understanding of the concepts, and increases retention of the material.

When it comes to eLearning, there isn't a live trainer and there aren't any classmates. How is a learner supposed to share the knowledge gained during class when the learner is alone? The answer is to add a quiz. In addition to having the ability to measure the effectiveness of the lesson, the students will be able to share what they have learned as they answer questions presented in the quiz.

Presenter includes a wonderful array of Question Types including Multiple Choice, True/False, Matching, Fill-in-the-blank, Hot Spot, and even Drag Drop. During the activities that follow, you'll get a chance to add a quiz and a few questions.

Student Activity: Add a Quiz

1. Using PowerPoint, open the **GrammarWithQuiz.pptx** file from the **Presenter11Data** folder.

   This presentation is similar to those you've worked with during several activities in this book with one notable exception: this one includes a quiz.

2. Preview the presentation.

   When you get near the end of the presentation, you'll be prompted to take a quiz. The quiz includes some of the Question Types mentioned above.

3. When finished taking the quiz, close the Preview.

4. Close the presentation (don't save if prompted).

5. Using PowerPoint, open the **QuizMe.pptx** file from the **Presenter11Data** folder.

6. Add a Quiz.

   ❏ from the Adobe Presenter tab, **Quiz** group, click the **Add Quiz** tool

   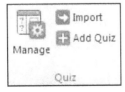

   The **New Quiz** dialog box opens.

7. Name the Quiz.

   ☐ on the **Quiz Settings** tab, change the **Name** to **Grammar Quiz**

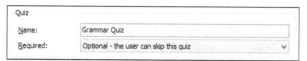

8. Enable specific Quiz Settings.

   ☐ from the **Settings** area, ensure **Allow backward movement**, **Allow user to review quiz** and **Show score at the end of quiz** are selected

The **Show score at the end of quiz** option will add a slide at the end of the quiz that will let the learners know how they did on the quiz. The **Allow backward movement** and **Allow user to review quiz** options will allow the learners to go back through the quiz and see which questions they got right or wrong (and if wrong, what the correct answer was).

☐ ensure the remaining options are deselected

Note: If you're curious about any of the other options, you can click the Help link in the lower left of the dialog box for detailed information.

9. Review the Question and Quiz Feedback Messages.

❑ click the **Question Review Messages** button

The Question Review Messages dialog box opens. As a learner answers questions, captions appear on the slide. Those captions rely on the text typed with this dialog box. The default text is fine, so you'll leave things as they are.

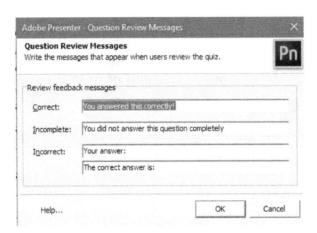

❑ click the **Cancel** button

❑ click the **Quiz Result Messages** button

The Quiz Result Messages dialog box opens. When the learner completes the quiz, a Quiz Results slide will appear containing the Pass or Fail messages typed here (along with the Score).

❑ change the **Pass** message to **Great job, you passed!**

❑ change the **Fail** message to **Sorry but you didn't pass. Better luck next time.**

❑ click the **OK** button (to close the Quiz Result Messages dialog box)

10. Set the Pass or Fail Options.

☐ still working in the **Quiz Settings** dialog box, click the **Pass or Fail Options** tab

You can set the Pass/Fail options to a percentage of correct answers needed to pass the quiz or a total number of points. The default is 80% or more of total score to pass. The default slide navigation is to Go to the next slide upon either a passing or failing grade. Other options include the ability to jump to a specific slide within the presentation or open a URL.

☐ change the **% or more of total score to pass** to **50**

☐ click the **OK** button

You are now back at the Quiz Manager dialog box. The new Grammar Quiz is listed on the Quizzes tab.

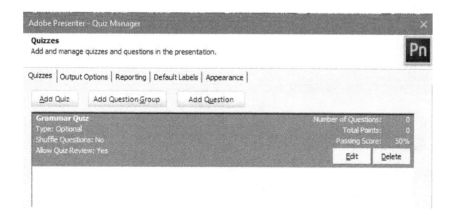

☐ click the **OK** button

Student Activity: Insert a Graded Question

1. Ensure that the **QuizMe** presentation is still open.

2. Add a Multiple Choice Question to the Grammar Quiz.

   ❏ select the **last slide** of the presentation

   ❏ from the Adobe Presenter tab, **Quiz** group, click the **Manage** tool

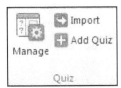

The Quiz Manager dialog box reopens.

   ❏ on the top of the **Quizzes** tab, click the **Add Question** button

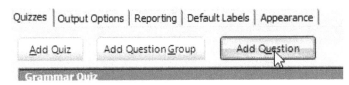

The Question Types dialog box opens.

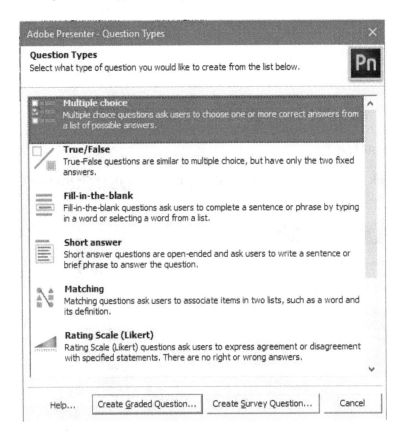

   ❏ ensure **Multiple choice** is selected

❏ click the **Create Graded Question** button

The **New multiple choice question** dialog box opens.

3. Add the Question.

   ❏ replace the existing question text with **Which of these words should be used as the subject of a sentence?**

4. Assign 50 points to the question.

   ❏ change the Score to **50**

5. Add the Answers.

   ❏ at the right of the dialog box, click the **Add** button

   ❏ type **Me** into the answer field

   ❏ click the **Add** button

   ❏ type **Myself** into the answer field

   ❏ click the **Add** button

   ❏ type **I** into the answer field

6. Select C as correct answer.

   ❏ at the left of answer **C**, select the radio button

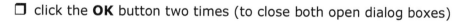

Question	Options	Reporting

Question

Name: Multiple choice

Question: Which of these words should be used as the subject of a sentence?

Score: 50

Answers

Select correct answer here ☐ Shuffle Answers

C A) Me   Add

C B) Myself   Delete

● C) I

Advanced...

   ❏ click the **OK** button two times (to close both open dialog boxes)

   Since you had selected slide 16 before you added the question slides, two slides are added to the end of the presentation. Slide 17 is the new Multiple Choice question; slide 18 is a Quiz Results slide.

7. Save your work.

Question Slide Confidence Check

1. Insert a True/False Question after slide 17 that looks like the image below:

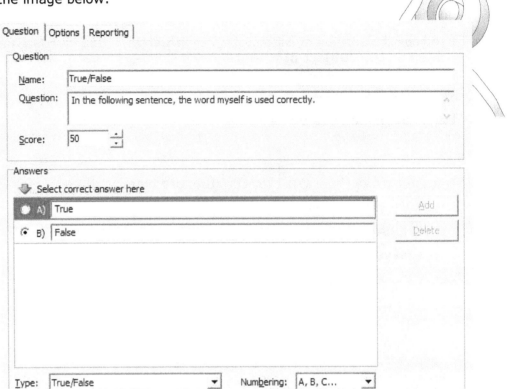

2. Select slide **17** and **Preview From Current Slide**.

3. Answer one of the Quiz Questions correctly and the other incorrectly.

   Since you set the **% or more of total score to pass** to 50%, you should be presented with a passing score on the Quiz Results slide.

4. Close the Preview window.

5. Save your work.

Student Activity: Add a Survey Question

1. Ensure that the **Quizme.pptx** presentation is still open.

2. Add a Rating Scale question to the Grammar Quiz.

   ❏ select slide **17**

   ❏ from the Adobe Presenter tab, **Quiz** group, click the **Manage** tool

   The Quiz Manager dialog box opens.

   ❏ from the top of the **Quizzes** tab, click the **Add Question** button

   The Question Types dialog box opens.

   ❏ select **Rating Scale (Likert)**

   ❏ click the **Create Survey Question** button

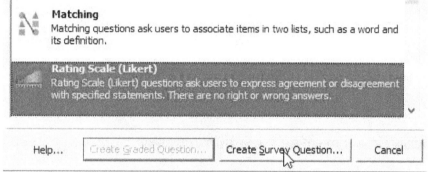

   ❏ in the Description area, ensure the text reads: **Indicate how strongly you agree or disagree with the following statements.**

   ❏ in the Questions area, click the **Add** button and type: **I feel confident I can use the pronouns me, myself, and I correctly.**

   ❏ click the **Add** button and type: **The quiz accurately reflected what was in the lesson.**

   ❏ click the **Add** button and type: **Samantha was an effective presenter.**

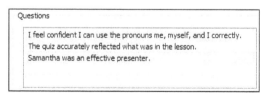

   ❏ in the **Answers** area, select **Disagree, Neutral**, and **Agree**

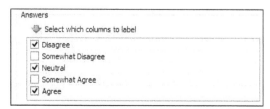

❒ click the **OK** button

The new Survey slide should look similar to the image below.

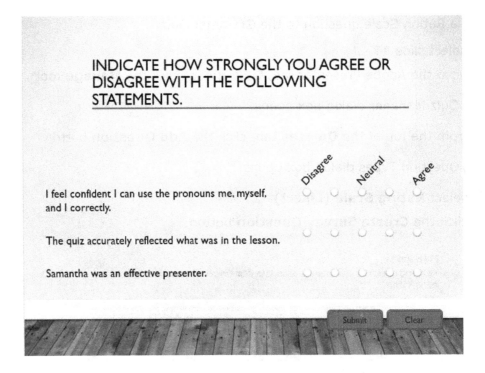

3. Select slide **17** and **Preview From Current Slide**.

4. Answer the questions as you get to them (it doesn't matter if you answer correctly or incorrectly).

5. Answer the Survey Question.

6. Close the Preview window.

7. Save and close the presentation.

iCONLOGiC

"Skills and Drills" Learning

Module 6: Reporting Data

In This Module You Will Learn About:

- Preparing a Lesson for an LMS, page 92
- Uploading to an LMS, page 100

And You Will Learn To:

- Set Quiz Reporting Options, page 93
- Create a Manifest File, page 96
- Publish a Content Package, page 98
- Create an Inquisiq LMS Account, page 101
- Create an LMS Course, page 103
- Attach a Lesson to a Course, page 104
- Create an LMS Catalog, page 106
- Attach a Course to a Catalog, page 107
- Test an eLearning Course, page 108

Preparing a Lesson for an LMS

Later in this module you will publish a presentation and then upload it into a Learning Management System (LMS) called Inquisiq. *But not so fast.* Before a lesson can be used with an LMS, you have to set up some reporting options and become familiar with the following: SCORM, AICC, SCOs, and the Manifest File.

SCORM

Developed by public- and private-sector organizations, Sharable Content Object Reference Model (SCORM) is a series of eLearning standards that specify ways to catalog, launch, and track course objects. Courses and management systems that follow the SCORM specifications allow for sharing of courses among federal agencies, colleges, and universities. Although SCORM is not the only eLearning standard (AICC is another), SCORM is one of the most common. There are two primary versions of SCORM—version 1.2, released in 1999, and version 2004.

AICC

Aviation Industry Computer-Based Training Committee (AICC) is an international association that develops guidelines for the aviation industry in the development, delivery, and evaluation of training technologies. When you publish your Presenter lessons, you can specify SCORM or AICC compliance, but not both. Not sure which one to pick? Talk to your LMS provider for information on which one to use. When in doubt, consider that AICC is older and more established than SCORM, but SCORM is the standard most often used today.

Tin Can API

Today's learners are consuming eLearning content using a vast array of devices (PCs, Macs, and mobile devices such as the iPad). And learners are working outside of traditional LMSs. In spite of these challenges, educators still need to capture reliable data about the learner experience.

The problem with data collection is that you need a place to store and access it. And your learners need live access to the storage area so that they can send the data. As mentioned above, the most widely used LMS standard for capturing data is SCORM. SCORM allows educators to track such things as learner completion of a course, pass/fail rates, and the amount of time a learner took to complete a lesson or course. But what if a trainer needs to get scores from learners who are collaborating with other students using social media? What if the learners don't have access to the Internet?

The new Tin Can API allows training professionals to gather detailed data about the learner experience as the learner moves through an eLearning course (either online or offline). According to the Tin Can API website, "The Tin Can API (sometimes known as the Experience API) captures data in a consistent format about a person or group's activities from many technologies. Very different systems are able to securely communicate by capturing and sharing this stream of activities using Tin Can's simple vocabulary."

If the Tin Can API is supported by your LMS, you'll be happy to learn that it's also fully supported in Adobe Presenter.

SCOs

Sharable Content Objects (SCOs) are standardized, reusable learning objects. An LMS can launch and communicate with SCOs and can interpret instructions that tell the LMS which SCO to show a user and when to show it. Why should you know what an SCO is? Actually, your Presenter projects are SCOs once you enable reporting (which you will learn to do next).

Manifest Files

The Manifest file allows your published presentation to be used and launched from a SCORM 1.2- or 2004-compliant LMS. When you publish a presentation, you can have Presenter create the Manifest file for you. The Manifest file that Presenter creates contains XML tags that describe the organization and structure of the published project to the LMS.

Student Activity: Set Quiz Reporting Options

1. Using PowerPoint, open the **GrammarWithQuiz.pptx** file from the **Presenter11Data** folder.

2. Enable Quiz Reporting for the presentation.

   ❐ from the Adobe Presenter tab, **Quiz** group, click the **Manage** tool

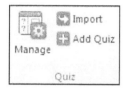

The Quiz Manager dialog box opens. On the **Quizzes** tab, notice that there is a quiz in the presentation containing four questions. The total value of the quiz is 100 points, and you need 75% or better to pass.

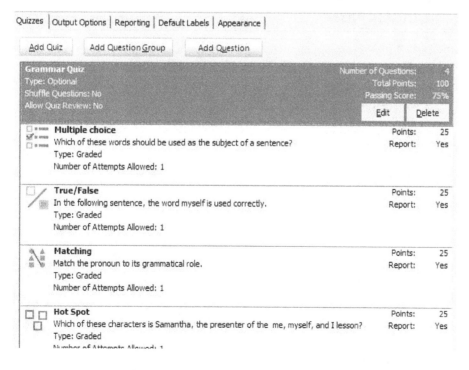

   ❐ select the **Reporting** tab

☐ select **Enable reporting for this presentation**

☐ from the **Learning Management System (LMS)** area, select **SCORM**

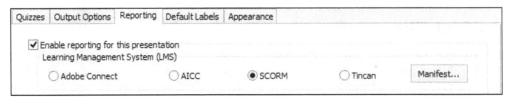

3. Set the Status Representation options.

☐ from the **Status Representation** area, select **Incomplete --->
Passed/Failed**

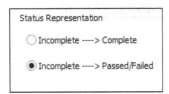

When the learner accesses the lesson through the LMS and takes the quiz, the score will be reported to the LMS; after the learner takes the quiz, the LMS displays Passed or Failed to the learner.

4. Set the Success/Completion Criteria.

☐ from the **Success/Completion Criteria** area, select **Slide views and/or quiz**

☐ select **Slide Views** and change the percentage to **100**

☐ select **Quiz is passed**

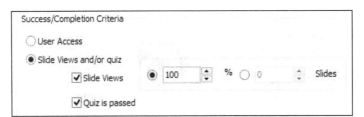

This setting will display a message to the learner that they've completed the lesson *and* passed the quiz.

5. Set the Data to report.

   ❑ from the **Data To Report** area, select **Quiz Score**

   ❑ from the **Quiz score** area, select **percentage**

   ┌───┐
   │ Data To Report   │
   │   ◉ Quiz Score   ○ Quiz Score + Interaction Data   │
   │   │
   │   Quiz Score : ◉ percentage   ○ points   │
   └───┘

   When the learner finishes with the lesson, the LMS will display the Quiz score as a percentage.

6. Leave the Quiz Manager open for the next activity.

Student Activity: Create a Manifest File

1. Ensure that the **GrammarWithQuiz** presentation is still open (the Quiz Manager dialog box should also still be open via **Adobe Presenter > Quiz group > Manage**).

2. Show the Manifest file options.

   ❏ from the top of **Reporting** tab, click the **Manifest** button

   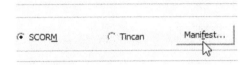

   The Manifest dialog box opens.

   ❏ from the SCORM Version drop-down menu, ensure **1.2** is selected

   SCORM 1.2, while an older standard, is still used by many LMS vendors today. In fact, Inquisiq (the LMS you will use shortly) supports SCORM 1.2, SCORM 2004, and AICC.

3. Set up the course information.

   ❏ in the **Identifier** field, type **grammar_course_001**

   The Identifier specifies a name used by the LMS to identify different manifests.

   ❏ in the **Title** field, type **Grammar Guide**

   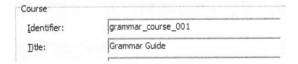

   The Title is seen by learners as they access the lesson on the LMS. Although you must add a Title here, the option is not supported in every LMS. In that case, any Title you add is ignored by the LMS.

   A Description is not required. Depending on the LMS you use, the text may or may not appear in the LMS. If the feature is not supported by the LMS, it will likely be ignored, just like the Title. You'll leave the Description blank for this lesson.

   The Version number, which you left selected, can be used to distinguish manifests with the same identifier.

   There are two other optional choices in the Course area: Duration and Subject. Duration lets you show how long it takes to complete the Presenter lesson. Subject allows you to specify a short description. When the course is displayed via a browser like Internet Explorer, the text in the Subject field can be searched like any web page.

4. Set up the SCO information.

□ in the **Identifier** field, type grammar_course_SCO_001

The Identifier, which cannot contain spaces, specifies a name used by the LMS to identify different SCOs.

□ in the **Title** field, type **Me, Myself, and I**

The Title you just typed will appear within the LMS.

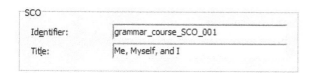

Note: If you would like information on the remaining options in this dialog box, click the **Help** link at the bottom left of the dialog box. At this point, the Manifest should look like the image below.

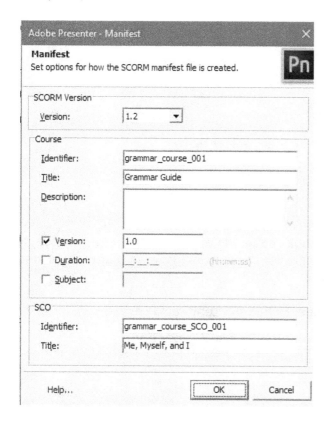

□ click the **OK** button to close the Manifest dialog box

□ click the **OK** button to close the Quiz Manager dialog box

5. Save your work.

Student Activity: Publish a Content Package

1. Ensure that the **GrammarWithQuiz** presentation is still open.

2. Specify a Location for the published lesson.

   ❏ from the Adobe Presenter tab, **Presentation** group, click the **Publish** tool

   The Publish Presentation dialog box opens.

   ❏ from the **Location** area, click the **Choose** button

   ❏ navigate to **Presenter11Data** and open the **PublishedLessons** folder

   ❏ click the **OK** button

3. Publish as both SWF and HTML5.

   ❏ From the **Publish Format** area, select **Both**

   You learned earlier in this book (page 24) why you might choose SWF, HTML5, or both as the Publish Format. Given the ever-growing popularity of mobile devices, the suggested option is Both.

4. Publish the presentation as a Zipped Content Package.

   ❏ from the **Output Options** area, select **Zip package**

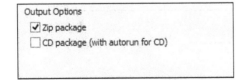

   ❏ click the **Publish** button

LMS Confidence Check

1. Save and close **GrammarWithQuiz** presentation.

2. **Minimize** PowerPoint and open the **Presenter11Data** folder.

3. Open the **PublishedLessons** folder.

   Locate the **GrammarWithQuiz.zip** file that you just Published. You'll be uploading this file into an LMS next.

   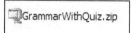

Uploading to an LMS

As mentioned earlier, LMS stands for Learning Management System. An LMS handles issues related to providing access to the content, delivery of the content, and student performance tracking/reporting. In short, an LMS is the backbone of a web-based training system.

Inquisiq

Inquisiq is an easy-to-use LMS created by ICS Learning Group (ICS). ICS (**www.icslearninggroup.com**) is a leading provider of computer-based training solutions including custom content development, LMS implementation, and instructional design. In addition, ICS specializes in corporate communications and multimedia development for touch-screen kiosks, interactive media, corporate websites, and online content management systems.

During the next few activities, you will be guided through the steps necessary to access Inquisiq, set up a user account, upload a content package, and create a Course and Curriculum. When you have completed this book, you will have up to 30 days to continue using Inquisiq free of charge. At the end of the evaluation period, you can purchase the LMS directly from ICS if you'd like to continue using their LMS.

Course Catalogs

A Course Catalog, also known as a Curriculum, is the plan you develop that details what your learners need to know when taking your courses, assets needed to implement the plan, and the context in which learning and teaching take place. The Curriculum sets the methods, structure, organization, balance, and presentation of the courses.

Courses

Each course you create serves as a building block of the Curriculum. Courses as they relate to learning are a series of lessons or steps that, when completed, fulfill the plan specified by the Curriculum. Each of the following could be considered a course: lectures, discussions, simulations, assignments, tests, and exams.

> **Note:** You must have Internet access to complete the remaining activities in this module. You will be setting up a free account on Inquisiq and will be able to use it for the next 30 days.

> Because Inquisiq is a web-based application and IconLogic does not have control over how or when the software is updated, some of the book's steps and or screen shots may not match what you see when you use Inquisiq. Nevertheless, the options/settings described in this book should still be similar enough that with some minor adjustments on your part, you can move forward.

Student Activity: Create an Inquisiq LMS Account

1. Create a user account in Inquisiq.

   ❑ using a web browser go to **https://www.inquisiq.com**

   ❑ at the top of the page, click the **Free Trial** link

   The Inquisiq LMS Free Trial Account page opens.

2. Specify a Domain Name and Password.

   ❑ fill in the Portal Name with your first and last name (the name you enter here will become part of the domain name used for your account... you can use **any name**, but **no spaces**)

   ❑ fill in the **Password** as you see fit

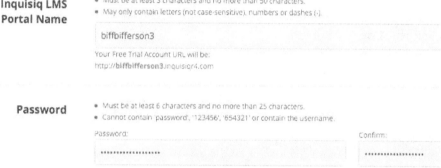

   ❑ continue to fill in the required fields (Name, Company Name, and Email) and agree to the User Agreements

   ❑ click the **Create My Free Trial** button

   Once the trial account has been set up, a confirmation screen opens. Take note of the Administrator Login Information. Your username is **administrator**. To test the system as a learner, you've also been assigned a username of **learner** and a password of **inquisiq**.

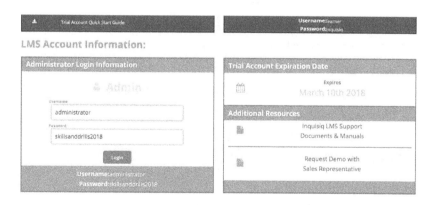

   ❑ from the top of the page, click the **URL** link to open the LMS

   Inquisiq LMS URL: http://biffbifferson3.inquisiqr4.com

3. Login to the LMS.

❏ at the far right of the screen, click the **Log In** button

❏ type **administrator** into the Username field

❏ type your administrator **password** into the Password field

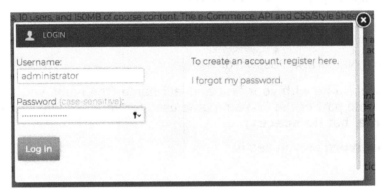

❏ click the **Log In** button

4. Upload a SCORM Package.

❏ from the **Content** area at the bottom of the page, click **SCORM Packages**

SCORM
PACKAGES

The SCORM Packages screen appears.

❏ from the SCORM Packages area, click the **Upload SCORM Package** link

The Upload screen appears.

❏ click the **Choose File** button

❏ navigate to the **Presenter11Data > PublishedLessons** folder

❏ open the **GrammarWithQuiz.zip** file you created during the last activity

Choose File | GrammarWithQuiz.zip

❏ click the **Upload** button

The package is imported into the LMS.

Package has been imported to the repository.

❏ click the **Close** button

Student Activity: Create an LMS Course

1. Ensure that you are still logged into your Inquisiq account.

2. Create a new course.

   ❏ from the top of the window, click the **Administrator Menu** link

   ❏ from the **Content** area at the bottom of the page, click **Courses**

   COURSES

   The Courses pages appears.

   ❏ from the top of the page, click **New Course**

   Courses ⊕ New Course

   ❏ in the **Name** field, name the new course **Grammar Guide**

   ❏ in the **Short Description** field, type **These interactive lessons will teach you the fundamentals of grammar.**

Code:	
*Name:	Grammar Guide
Rating:	☑ Enable ratings for this course.
Estimated Length:	___ hour(s) and ___ minute(s)
*Short Description:	(Maximum 512 Characters)
	These interactive lessons will teach you the fundamentals of grammar.

   ❏ from the bottom of the page, click the **Save Changes** button

   Success

   Course has been saved successfully.

   ⊘ OK

   ❏ click the **OK** button

Student Activity: Attach a Lesson to a Course

1. Ensure that you are still logged into your Inquisiq account.

2. Attach a Content Package (SCO) to a course.

   ☐ from the top of the window, click the **Administrator Menu** link

   ☐ from the Content area at the bottom of the page, click **Courses**

   COURSES

   The Grammar Guide course is listed among the default courses.

   ☐ click the name of the course

   The course opens for editing.

   ☐ click the **Lessons** tab

   ☐ click **New Lesson**

   The New Lesson window appears.

   ☐ in the **Name** field, name the lesson **Me, Myself, and I**

   ☐ in the **Short Description** field, type **This lesson will teach you the correct use of the pronouns Me, Myself, and I.**

   Complete the form below to add or update the properties of this lesson.

   Required items are marked with an asterisk (*).

* Name:	Me, Myself, and I
* Type:	Online Lesson ⬍
	[None Selected] / [None Selected]
	Select Package/Resource
* Short Description:	*(Maximum 512 Characters)*
	This lesson will teach you the correct use of the pronouns Me, Myself, and I.

   ⊘ Save Changes   ⊗ Cancel

❑ click the **Select Package/Resource** button

The Packages window opens. This is where you find any content packages that you have uploaded to the LMS. In this instance, you see your GrammarWithQuiz.zip package that you uploaded earlier, along with several assets that are included with the Inquisiq trial account.

❑ select the **GrammarWithQuiz.zip** package

001-active-listening.zip
001-quicksell.zip
002-creating-great-customer-conversations.zip
002-how-to-be-a-great-conversationalist.zip
013-becoming-a-great-leader-introduction.zip
120035.zip
160045.zip
GrammarWithQuiz.zip

⊘ Select Package   ⊗ Close Window

❑ click the **Select Package** button

❑ select **grammar_course_sco_001_RES**

grammar_course_SCO_001_RES

You gave the SCO this name when you set up the Manifest on page 97.

❑ click the **Select Resource** button

❑ click the **Save Changes** button and then close the Lesson window

3. Publish an LMS Course.

❑ from the top of the window, click the **Administrator Menu** link

❑ from the bottom of the window, click **Courses**

❑ from the far left, click the **check mark** for the **Grammar Guide** course

❑ from the **Options** column, click the **gray check mark**

Course is not Published - Click to Publish

❑ click **OK** to confirm that you want to publish the course

Once the course is published, the gray check mark turns green. The final steps are to create a Catalog and attach the Grammar Guide course to the catalog so that it can be accessed by your online learners.

▉ Grammar Guide

Student Activity: Create an LMS Catalog

1. Ensure that you are still logged into your Inquisiq account.

2. Add a Catalog (Curriculum) to the LMS.

☐ from the top of the window, click the **Administrator Menu** link

☐ from the bottom of the screen, click **Course Catalog**

☐ click **New Catalog**

COURSE CATALOG

📖 New Catalog

The New Catalog window appears.

☐ in the **Name** area, type **Writing and Grammar**

☐ in the **Short Description** area, type **These courses will teach you some best practices when writing step-by-step documentation.**

* Name:	Writing and Grammar
* Privacy:	◉ Public ○ Private
* Allow Self-Enrollment:	○ Yes ◉ No 💬 Yes' enables learners to enroll in this catalog as a single transaction based on the pricing option you select below.
* Short Description:	*(Maximum 512 Characters)* These courses will teach you some best practices when writing step-by-step documentation.

☐ scroll down and click the **Save Changes** button

☐ close the Catalog window

The new **Writing and Grammar** catalog now appears in the Course Catalogs menu.

⊿ ◌ Course Catalogs:
  - 📄 Business Skills - Sample Courses
  - 📄 Industrial Manufacturing - Sample Courses
  - 📄 Inquisiq Overview Courses
  - 📄 Writing and Grammar
  - 📄 Becoming a Great Leader: Introduction
  - 📄 Grammar Guide

Student Activity: Attach a Course to a Catalog

1. Ensure that you are still logged into your Inquisiq account.

2. Attach a course to a catalog.

   ☐ select the **Writing and Grammar** Catalog

   ☐ at the right of the Catalog list, click **Add Course(s) To Catalog**

   📖 New Catalog

   ✏ Modify This Catalog

   ❌ Delete This Catalog

   📖 Add Course(s) To Catalog

   The Courses window appears. The Grammar Guide course you added is included in the list along with other courses included in the Inquisiq trial account.

   ☐ select the **Grammar Guide** course

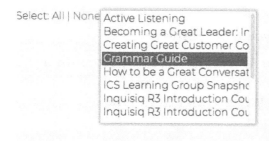

Select: All | None   Active Listening
Becoming a Great Leader: In
Creating Great Customer Co
Grammar Guide
How to be a Great Conversat
ICS Learning Group Snapshc
Inquisiq R3 Introduction Cou
Inquisiq R3 Introduction Cou

✓ OK

   ☐ click the **OK** button twice

   The Grammar Guide course has been added to the Writing and Grammar catalog.

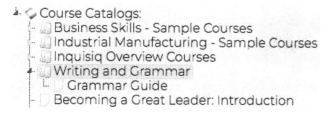

📚 Course Catalogs:
  📘 Business Skills - Sample Courses
  📘 Industrial Manufacturing - Sample Courses
  📘 Inquisiq Overview Courses
  📘 Writing and Grammar
    📄 Grammar Guide
  📄 Becoming a Great Leader: Introduction

Student Activity: Test an eLearning Course

1. Logout of the LMS.

   ☐ at the upper right of the LMS window, click the **Log Out** button

   You cannot test the lesson while logged in as an administrator. The Inquisiq trial account includes a "learner" account that allows you to test the course.

2. Login to the LMS using the learner account.

   ☐ at the upper right of the LMS window, click the **Log In** button

   ☐ type **learner** into the **Username** field

   ☐ in the **Password** field, type **inquisiq**

   Because this is the first time you are using the "learner" account, you are required to create a new password.

   ☐ type any password you like (you can use the same password that you used when you created the administrator account, but keep the password in mind should you want to access the account later)

   ☐ after you have changed the password, click the **Change Password** button

   ☐ click the **Close** button

3. Test the Grammar Guide course you added earlier.

   ☐ at the top of the window, hover above the words **My Account** and choose **Course Catalog**

   ☐ from the list of Catalogs, click **Writing and Grammar**

   📖 Catalog: Writing and Grammar

   Courses: 1

   These courses will teach you some best practices when writing step-by-step documentation.

   The Grammar Guide course you created, published, and attached to the catalog is the only course available. In a real catalog, there would likely be multiple courses each containing multiple lessons.

   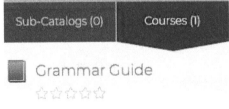

   ☐ click the **Grammar Guide** course title

❏ click the **Enroll Now** button

❏ click the **My Account** link to launch the course

The Grammar Guide course is available in the list of Learning Activities.

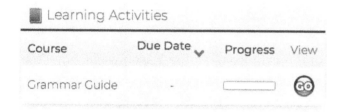

❏ click the green **Go** button to access the course

Notice that the status of the **Me, Myself, and I** lesson **Status** is **Not Attempted**.

Title	Status	Score	Action
1. Me, Myself, and I	Not Attempted	-	GO

❏ click the green **Go** button to start the lesson

The lesson plays in its own window.

4. When you get to the quiz, go ahead and work through it. (It doesn't matter if you pass it or not—so no worries.)

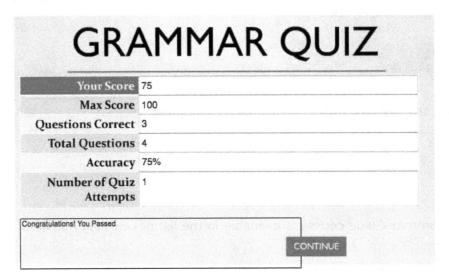

5. When you reach the end of the course, close the lesson window. (After the window closes, the LMS saves the data.)

6. Click the words **Click here to go back to the course details page**.

Data Saved.

Click here to go back to the course details page.

And like magic, the status of the lesson changes from **Not Attempted** to either **Passed** or **Failed**.

Learning Activities

Title	Status	Score	Action
▶ 1. Me, Myself, and I	Passed	75%	🔘

7. Logout of the LMS.

    ❏ click the **Log Out** link in the upper right of the window

At this point, you can close the web browser.

iCONLOGiC

"Skills and Drills" Learning

Module 7: Finishing Touches

In This Module You Will Learn About:

- Themes, page 112
- Settings, page 116
- Managing Slides, page 120
- Packaging, page 124

And You Will Learn To:

- Apply a Theme, page 112
- Customize a Theme, page 114
- Edit the Presentation Settings, page 116
- Add a Presenter, page 118
- Modify Sidebar Presenter Info, page 119
- Assign a Presenter to Slides, page 120
- Create a Package, page 124

Themes

Themes perform much the same function for a Presenter presentation as your clothes perform for you. Bored? Bummed? Perhaps something simple like changing your clothes would be enough to change your attitude. Consider some of the top websites in the world. During the holiday season, sites like amazon.com and google.com change the whole attitude of their site just by changing the "skin" used on their sites to reflect the season. The sites themselves don't change, just the outer skin changes.

You are about to learn how easy it is to change the skin used by your presentation. And you will learn that Themes can be customized to suit your taste—you can select from several playbars, buttons, and color schemes.

Student Activity: Apply a Theme

1. Using PowerPoint, open the **PublishPackageMe.pptx** file from the **Presenter11Data** folder.

2. Starting on slide **2**, preview the Next 5 slides.

   As the preview moves along, notice the appearance of the playbar at the bottom of the lesson. On slide 2, you'll hear the presenter speaking, but the Sidebar video is missing along with a TOC that will allow learners to skip to different parts of the lesson.

3. Close the preview.

4. Apply a Theme.

   ❏ from the Adobe Presenter tab, **Theme** group, click the **Theme** tool

   The Theme Editor opens.

   ❏ from the **Theme** drop-down menu, choose **Mojave**

Options within the Theme Editor change dramatically. Among other things, the Mojave theme includes a specific color scheme, a Sidebar at the far right of the window, Presenter Info, and Panes.

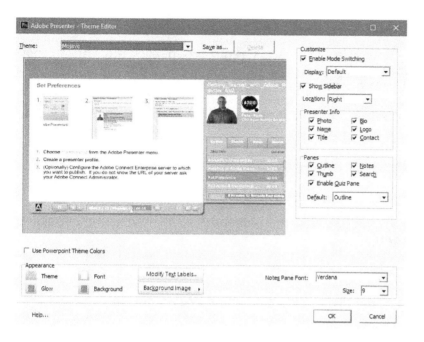

❑ click the **OK** button to close the Theme Editor dialog box

5. Starting on slide **2**, preview the Next 5 slides.

You can now see the Sidebar video that you learned to add on page 59. However, the presenter ends up pointing to the wrong side of the screen. The video will work better if the sidebar is on the other side of the screen.

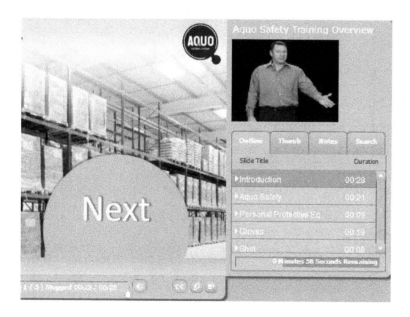

6. Close the preview.

Student Activity: Customize a Theme

1. Ensure that the **PublishPackageMe.pptx** presentation is still open.

2. Customize a Theme.

   ☐ from the Adobe Presenter tab, **Theme** group, click the **Theme** tool

   The Theme Editor opens again.

   ☐ from the **Customize** area, **Location** drop-down menu, choose **Left**

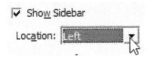

   The preview area shows that the Sidebar is positioned at the left side of the lesson window.

3. Save the Theme.

   ☐ at the top of the dialog box, click the **Save as** button

   The Save as dialog box opens.

   ☐ in the **Name** field, type **AquoTheme**

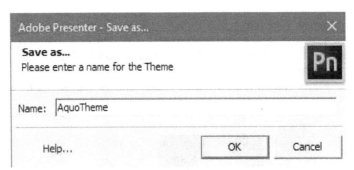

   ☐ click the **OK** button

   ☐ click the **OK** button to close the Theme Editor

4. Starting on slide **2**, preview the Next 5 slides.

   Notice that the Sidebar now appears at the left and the problem with the video guide pointing in the wrong direction has been resolved.

5. Close the preview.

Themes Confidence Check

1. Return to the Theme Editor and apply some of the other Themes to the presentation.

2. Preview the slides if you'd like to see how the Theme works with the presentation.

3. Apply the **AquoTheme** to the presentation.

4. Save your work.

Settings

The Theme that you just learned how to apply to a presentation has an option to add information about the presenter including the Name, Title, and Contact information. The information used in the Theme comes from information added to the Settings dialog box. In addition to the presenter's information, you can also use the Settings dialog box to add such things as a Title to the presentation, set the Audio Quality used in the published lesson, and the Image quality.

Student Activity: Edit the Presentation Settings

1. Ensure that the **PublishPackageMe.pptx** presentation is still open.

2. Add a Title to the presentation.

   ❐ from the Adobe Presenter tab, **Tools** group, click the **Settings** tool

   The Settings dialog box opens.

   ❐ from the list of Settings at the left of the dialog box, click **Appearance**

   ❐ ensure that the **Title** is **Aquo Safety Training Review**

   The Title will appear above the Sidebar when you Preview or Publish the lesson.

3. Set the hardware target.

   ❐ from the list of Settings at the left of the dialog box, select **Quality**

   ❐ from the **Publish For** drop-down menu, ensure **My Computer** is selected

   There are four Publish For options: My Computer, Adobe Connect Pro, Adobe PDF, and Adobe Captivate Prime. The most common selection is My Computer. You would change the setting to **Connect Pro** if you were publishing to the Adobe Connect Pro server and Adobe PDF if you were primarily creating PDFs.

   Note: Adobe Captivate Prime is Adobe's top-of-the-line Learning Management System.

4. Set the Audio and Image Quality in the Published lesson.

❑ from the **Audio Quality** area, select **Low Bandwidth**

While selecting CD Quality would *potentially* result in the best sound, your learner needs high-end speakers to enjoy the quality. As a general rule, FM Quality is more than adequate for audio that is played through typical computer speakers or headsets. And Low Bandwidth is typically pretty good too. Keep in mind that using CD Quality or Near CD Quality results in larger published lessons than either FM Quality or Low Bandwidth.

❑ from the **Image Quality** area, select **Medium**

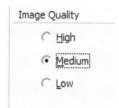

As with Audio, selecting High as the Image Quality will result in a larger published lesson. Typically, the Medium selection is the best balance between file size and image quality. However, you may need to experiment with the Image Quality options. If you Publish a lesson using the Medium or Low settings and the slide backgrounds look grainy, you'll need to return to this dialog box and try Publishing using the High setting.

Note: If you select **Use these settings for new presentations** (located at the bottom of the dialog box), future projects will use the same Quality settings.

❑ click the **OK** button

Student Activity: Add a Presenter

1. Ensure that the **PublishPackageMe.pptx** presentation is still open.

2. Add a Presenter to the presentation.

   ❏ from the Adobe Presenter tab, **Tools** group, click the **Settings** tool

   ❏ from the **Application** category at the left, click **Presenters**

   ❏ if there are any Presenters listed in the dialog box, select them and then click the **Delete** button (in the lower right of the dialog box)

   ❏ click the **Add** button

   The Presenter dialog box opens.

   ❏ in the **Name** field, type **Jim Stevens**

   ❏ in the **Job Title** field, type **Safety Manager**

   ❏ in the **Email** field, type **jim.stevens@aquo.com**

   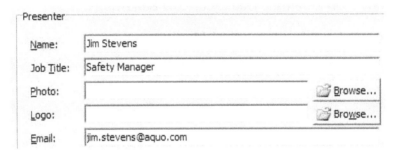

   ❏ click the **OK** button

   The new Presenter appears in the Presenters area.

   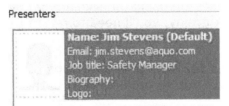

   ❏ click the **OK** button

3. Save the presentation.

Student Activity: Modify Sidebar Presenter Info

1. Ensure that the **PublishPackageMe.pptx** presentation is still open.

2. Control the information that appears on the Sidebar.

   ❏ from the Adobe Presenter tab, **Theme** group, click the **Theme** tool

   The Theme Editor opens again.

   ❏ at the right side of the **Theme Editor**, **Presenter Info** area, remove the check mark from **Photo**, **Bio**, and **Logo**

   ❏ click the **OK** button

3. Beginning on slide **2**, preview the **Next 5 Slides**.

   While the Presenter Info does not yet appear at the left, the Title you edited a few minutes ago does.

   Next you'll assign a Presenter to most of the slides. Once you do that, the Presenter Info will appear on the Sidebar.

4. Close the Preview.

Managing Slides

You use the Slide Manager to specify a Presenter for an individual slide (or a group of slides), add a Navigation Name (the name that appears in the Sidebar), allow for user interactivity, control slide jumps, hide or show the Playbar, and get an overview of the multimedia assets that have been added to a slide.

Student Activity: Assign a Presenter to Slides

1. Ensure that the **PublishPackageMe.pptx** presentation is still open.

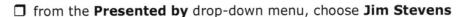

2. Assign Jim Stevens as the Presenter for a single slide.

   ❑ from the Adobe Presenter tab, **Tools** group, click **Slide Manager**

   The Slide Manager dialog box opens.

   ❑ select Slide **2**

   ❑ from the **Presented by** drop-down menu, choose **Jim Stevens**

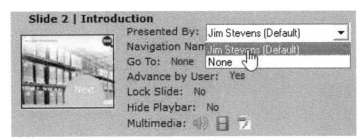

3. Assign Jim Stevens as the Presenter to multiple slides.

   ❑ at the bottom left of the Slide Manager dialog box, click **Select All**

   ❑ click the **Edit** button

   The Edit Multiple Slides dialog box opens.

   ❑ from the **Presented By** drop-down menu, choose **Jim Stevens**

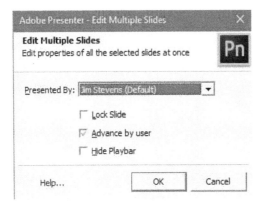

   ❑ click the **OK** button

Notice that every slide in the Slide Manager now shows Jim Stevens as the presenter.

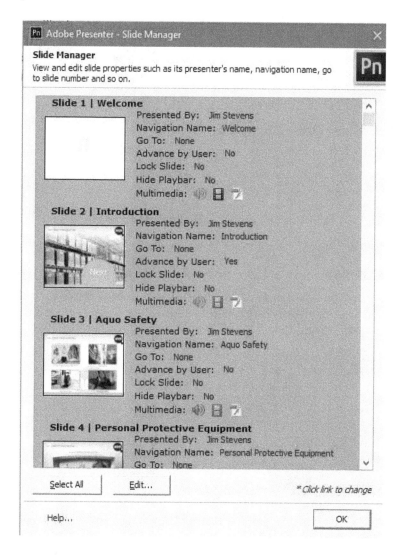

4. Change the Navigation Name for a slide.

☐ still working within the Slide Manager, scroll down to Slide **6**

☐ click within the current Navigation Name and change the name to **Shirts**

Slide 6 | Shirts

Presented By: Jim Stevens
Navigation Name: Shirts
Go To: None

☐ click the **OK** button to close the Slide Manager dialog box

5. Save your work.

Slide Manager Confidence Check

1. Open the Slide Manager dialog box.

2. Change the presenter for Slide 1 to **None**.

Slide 1 | Welcome

Presented By: None
Navigation Name: Welcome
Go To: None
Advance by User: No
Lock Slide: No
Hide Playbar: No
Multimedia: 🔊 🎞 📽

3. Change the Navigation Name for Slide 7 to **Hard Hats**.

4. Change the Navigation Name for Slide 9 to **Goggles**.

5. Preview the presentation.

Notice that the presenter info appears for every slide except slide 1. And if you use the Outline panel to scroll through the presentation, you can see the Navigation Names you added.

Notice that there is a Notes tab. Had you added Notes to the PowerPoint slides, those Notes would appear on the Notes tab should learners either click the Notes tab on the TOC, or click the CC button on the playbar. Let's see how that works.

6. Close the Preview.

7. On slide 1, click in the **Notes** area.

8. Type **Welcome to today's presentation**.

Welcome to today's training presentation.

≜ Notes

9. On slide 2, click in the Notes area.

10. Type **Hi, I'm Jim Stevens and this is just a test of how notes typed in PowerPoint's Notes area can appear on the notes tab and serve as closed captions.**

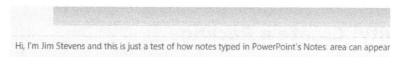

Hi, I'm Jim Stevens and this is just a test of how notes typed in PowerPoint's Notes area can appear

11. Preview the presentation again.

12. Either click the **Notes** tab or the **CC** button on the playbar to see the text you typed into the Notes area of the first two slides.

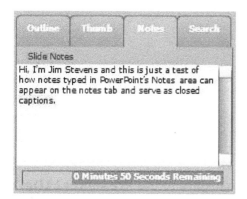

If you wanted to make quick work out of adding Notes/Closed Captions to a project, transcribing the text yourself is the last thing you'd want to do. If you created a voiceover script prior to starting work in Presenter, you'd be able to copy/paste the text from the script into PowerPoint's Notes panel. Alternatively, you can hire transcription services to convert existing audio into text-based files and save yourself the work of typing the text yourself. One transcription service we've used with great success is Rev (www.rev.com).

13. Close the Preview.

Packaging

If you need to share your Adobe Presenter presentation with another developer, you'll find the Package tool very useful. Presenter projects begin as a single, self-contained PowerPoint presentation. You can transfer them from one computer to another without worrying about leaving a part of the presentation behind. However, once you add audio or videos assets to a slide, those assets aren't embedded into the presentation. Instead, Presenter creates a folder that houses those assets every time you save. Should you forget to include the assets folder when you send the PowerPoint presentation to a colleague, the person opening the presentation will receive messages about missing files as Presenter attempts to find the assets. When you Package a Presenter project, everything a developer needs to open the project is included in the package (except for the Microsoft PowerPoint or Adobe Presenter software). A developer simply needs to double-click the PRPKG file they receive from you to extract all of the project assets into a new folder.

Student Activity: Create a Package

1. Ensure that the **PublishPackageMe.pptx** presentation is still open.

2. Create a Package.

    ❏ from the Adobe Presenter tab, **Presentation** group, click the **Package** tool

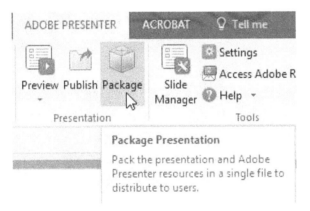

The Package dialog box opens.

    ❏ click the **Browse** button [...] and navigate to the **Presenter11Data** folder
    ❏ click the **Save** button

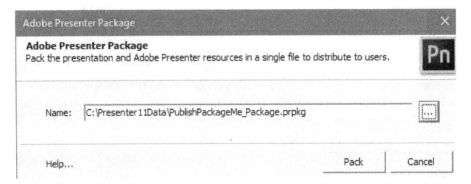

    ❏ click the **Pack** button and then click the **OK** button

Your Final Confidence Check

1. **Minimize** PowerPoint and open the **Presenter11Data** folder.

2. Locate the package that you just created.

   Note: You can send the package to another Presenter developer and they'll have everything they need to open and edit the presentation.

3. Return to PowerPoint.

4. Publish the presentation as both **SWF and HTML5** to the PublishedLessons folder for **My Computer**, and again as a **PDF** (you learned how to publish a presentation using both of these output options beginning on page 24).

5. Save and close the presentation.

Notes

Index

A

A. Dawn Shaikh, 6
About the Author, vi
Add Question button, 86
Add Silence, 47
Adjust volume, 50
Adobe, 2
Adobe Captivate Prime, 116
Adobe Connect, 24
Adobe Connect Pro, 116
Adobe Flash Player, 24
Adobe PDF, 25, 116
Adobe Presenter
    Interface, 20
Adobe Presenter tab, 21
Adobe Software Updates, ix
Advance by User, 71, 72
AICC, 92
Allow backward
    movement, 83
Allow user to review quiz, 83
Arial, 4, 5
Association of Information
    Systems, 4
Attach a Lesson to a
    Course, 104
Audio
    Free downloads, 44
    MP3, 44
    WAV, 44
Audio Quality, 117
Audio value, 16
Audio Volume, 50
Auto Capture versus Manual
    Capture, 7

B

Barbara S. Chaparro, 6
Book Conventions, vi
Branching, 78

C

Calibri, 5
CC button, 123
CD Quality, 117
Century Schoolbook, 5
Characters, 30
Closed Captions, 123
Connect Pro, 116
Content Package, 98
Course Catalogs, 100
Courses, 100
Create an LMS Course, 103
Create Survey Question
    button, 89

D

Data Files, download from

the Web, viii
Data To Report, 95
Death by PowerPoint, 2
Delete Audio, 47
Designing Slides, 3
Doug Fox, 6

E

eCommerce, 4
Edit Link, 78
eLearning, 2
eLearning Budgeting
    Considerations, 8
E-Mail, ix
Experience API, 92
Explore an Existing
    Presentation, 20

F

Fail message, 84
Flash file, 24
Flash Player download
    page, 24
FM Quality, 117
Fonts, 4
Fonts and Learning, 4
Fonts, Most Popular, 5
FTP server, 24

G

Ganga Dhanesh, 4
Graded Questions,
    Adding, 86

H

Hardware target, 116
Helvetica, 5
HTML5, 24, 27, 98
Hyperlink, Create, 78
Hyperlink, Remove, 79

I

Image Quality, 117
Image Quality (when
    Published), 116
Images, Import, 61
Import Audio, 44
Inquisiq, 92, 100
Insert Interaction, 66
Insert Silence tool, 48
Interactions, 66
iOS, 24
iPad, 24

L

Learning Management
    System (LMS) area, 94
Likert, 89

Link, 78
LMS, 24, 92
    Add a
        Curriculum, 106, 107
    Course, 100
    Create a
        Course, 103, 104
    Create an Account, 101
    Curriculum, 100
    Inquisiq, 100
    Manifest File, 96
    SCO, 92
    SCORM, 92
    SCORM 1.2, 93
    Test an E-Learning
        Course, 108
    Test an eLearning
        Course, 108
LMS Catalog, 106
Low Bandwidth, 117

M

Manage a Slide, 71
Manage tool, 86
Manager
    Interactions, 67, 68, 74
Manifest, 93
Manifest
    File, 93, 112, 114, 116, 1
    24
Microphone placement, 41
Microphone technique, 41
Microsoft, 6
Mobile devices, 24
MP4, 55
MPEG Audio Layer III, 44
My Computer, 116

N

Near CD Quality, 117
New Quiz dialog box, 82
Notes, 123
Notes tab, 122

P

Pack, 124
Package, 124
Package, Create, 124
Packaging, 124
Palatino, 5
Pass message, 84
PDF, 24, 25
Personality traits, 6
Personas, Fonts, 6
Pictures, Import, 61
Planning eLearning
    Projects, 7
Planning New Movies, 7

Playhead, 45
Popular Fonts, 5
PowerPoint, 2
PowerPoint, Death by, 2
Presentation Settings, 116
Presentation Title (when
    Published), 116
Presenter, Add, 118
Presenter's Role, 2
Presenter9Data, viii, 20
Preview, 21
Production Excludes, 8
Production Includes, 8
PRPKG file, 124
Publish as Adobe PDF, 25
Publish Both, 27
Publish Format, 98
Publish Presentation dialog
    box, 24
Publish Presentations, 25
Publishing, 111

Q
Question Review
    Messages, 84
Question, Add, 86
QuickTime, 55
Quiz group, 23
Quiz is passed, 94
Quiz
    Manager, 93, 112, 114, 1
    24
        Choose Report Data, 95
        Enable reporting for this
            project, 93, 94
        Reporting Options, 93
        Set Reporting
            options, 95
        Set Reporting Status
            options, 94
Quiz Result Messages, 84
Quiz score, 95
Quiz Settings, 83
Quiz Settings tab, 83
Quiz, Add, 82

R
Rating Scale (Likert), 89
Readability of Fonts, 5
Readability of Fonts Affects
    Participation, 5

Record audio tool, 42
Recording Audio
    Microphone
        placement, 41
    Microphone
        technique, 41
    Setup, 41
Recording Voiceover
    Audio, 41
Resize an image, 31
Rev (inexpensive text
    transcription), 123

S
Sans Serif, 4
Scale height, 31
Scale width, 31
Scenario Interactions, 73
Scenes, 34
SCO Identifier, 97
SCORM, 94
SCOs, 92
Screen Resolution, 7
Scripts for Software
    Demonstrations, 10
Scripts in Paragraph
    Format, 10
Scripts in Table Format, 10
Select a correct answer, 87
Select File(s) to Import, 44
Send to Back, 62
Serif, 4
Settings, Presentation, 116
Sharable Content Object
    Reference Model, 92
Sharath Sasidharan, 4
Should Voiceover Audio
    Match the Screen
    Text?, 16
Show score at the end of
    quiz, 83
Show Sidebar, 60
Sidebar, 60
Sidebar Video, 59
Silence, 47
Skeptical audience, 4
Slide Manager, 71, 120
Slide Video, 55
Slide Views, 94
Slide, Advance by
    User, 71, 72

Soft Skills, 11
Software
    Demonstrations, 10
Status Representation
    area, 94
Storyboarding for Soft
    Skills, 11
Survey Question, Adding, 89
SWF, 24, 27, 98
System requirement for
    viewing Presenter
    content, viii
System requirements for
    Authoring, vii

T
Theme Editor, 60
Theme group, 59
Theme tool, 23, 59
Themes, 112
Themes, Customize, 114
Times, 5
Times New Roman, 5
Tin Can API, 92
Tools group, 116
Trust, Fonts, 4
Typography, 4

U
Upload SCORM Package, 102
Use these settings for new
    presentations, 117

V
Verdana, 4, 5
Video, 55
Video tool, 54
Video, Add, 54
Video, Edit, 55
Video, Sidebar, 59
View output after
    publishing, 28
View warning messages, 28
Voiceover Scripts, 38

W
WAVE, 44
Waveform, 45
Web server, 24
WinZip Self-Extractor, viii
Word Search Interaction, 66

www.ingramcontent.com/pod-product-compliance
Lightning Source LLC
Chambersburg PA
CBHW060149060326

40690CB00018B/4039